THICKER THAN WATER:

ONE-ACT PLAYS BY THE MEMBERS OF YOUNGBLOOD

HEIGHTS
by Amy Fox

WATERBORN
by Edith L. Freni

CHARLIE BLAKE'S BOAT
by Graeme Gillis

D.C.
by Daria Polatin

WELCOME BACK, BUDDY COMBS
by Ben Rosenthal

★

★

DRAMATISTS
PLAY SERVICE
INC.

D1569027

THICKER THAN WATER
Copyright © 2005, Ensemble Studio Theatre

All Rights Reserved

INTRODUCTION

Youngblood is the Ensemble Studio Theatre's collective of emerging professional playwrights under the age of thirty. Founded in 1993, Youngblood serves as a creative home for the next generation of theatre artists.

The writers come together for weekly meetings, readings and workshop productions, where they develop their craft, receive feedback and engage each other in professional collaborations. Each season, the group's most polished work is produced on the E.S.T. Mainstage. Over the past ten years, Youngblood has developed into a potent force in the theatre community.

Plays by Youngblood members have been produced at The Royal Court Theatre, South Coast Rep, Playwrights Horizons, Actors Theatre of Louisville, The Mark Taper Forum, Rattlestick Theatre, The New York International Fringe Festival, and have been optioned by film companies including Merchant Ivory. Alumni include Christopher Shinn, John Belluso, Lucy Thurber, Crystal Skillman, Jeremy Soule and Elyzabeth Gregory Wilder.

HEIGHTS was originally produced as a part of THICKER THAN WATER (2000) by Youngblood (Chris Smith, Artistic Director) and the Ensemble Studio Theatre (Curt Dempster, Founder/Artistic Director) at the Ensemble Studio Theatre in New York City in January 2000. It was directed by Jimmy Bohr; the set design was by Mike Allen; the costume design was by Kimberly Matela; the lighting design was by Shawn Gallagher; and the sound design was by Dean Gray. The cast was as follows:

ALEC .... Andersen Gabrych
ISABEL .... Sally Wheeler
JONATHAN .... Peter Rini

D.C., WATERBORN, CHARLIE BLAKE'S BOAT and WEL-COME BACK, BUDDY COMBS were produced as THICKER THAN WATER (2004) by Youngblood (J. Holtham and R.J. Tolan, Co-Artistic Directors) and the Ensemble Studio Theatre (Curt Dempster, Founder/Artistic Director) at the Ensemble Studio Theatre in New York City in March 2004. The set design was by Lex Liang; the costume design was by Amanda Embry; the lighting design was by Doug Filomena; and the sound design was by Robert Gould. The casts and directors were as follows:

WATERBORN by Edith L. Freni
Directed by Brian Roff
MARK .... Michael Szeles
LESLIE .... Annie McNamara

CHARLIE BLAKE'S BOAT by Graeme Gillis
Directed by Jamie Richards
HELEN .... Katie Barrett
CHARLIE .... Leo Lauer

D.C. by Daria Polatin
Directed by R.J. Tolan
MANDY .... Shana Dowdeswell
WILBUR .... Gideon Glick
MISS PASSIVO .... Joanna Parson

WELCOME BACK, BUDDY COMBS by Ben Rosenthal
Directed by Abigail Zealey Bess
BUDDY COMBS .... Johnny Giacalone
BEVERLY COMBS .... Diana Ruppe
WYNNE FRANKLIN .... Denny Bess

CONTENTS

HEIGHTS
by Amy Fox

CHARACTERS

ALEC, a man in his early 20s

ISABEL, a woman in her early 20s

JONATHAN, a man in his early 20s

HEIGHTS

The rooftop of a city apartment. Night. The surrounding apartment buildings can be seen, many of their windows lit. There is a door leading to stairs inside the apartment building. Isabel is lying on a deck chair, half-asleep. She has headphones on and a large sweatshirt draped over her. Alec enters, speaking on his cell phone. He is also carrying a bottle of wine, two glasses and several candles. Isabel's chair is off to the side and turned away from Alec, and he does not notice her. As he speaks, Alec sets a bottle of wine and two glasses on a small iron table, and places the candles carefully. Isabel notices him and watches, removing her headphones.

ALEC.   Right, sesame chicken, imperial chicken, right, and steamed dumplings. Well, I'm on the roof. The roof. The top, right. Well you've come up here before. We've done this before. A few weeks ago, you sent the guy up here, right. Okay. Okay fine. We'll come down. Okay, in the lobby, okay. No, don't call. Don't call me up here. We'll come down, let's say three o'clock, we'll come down. Right. *(Alec hangs up the phone and puts it in his coat pocket. He attempts to light the candles, but without much success.)* Come on now. Come on. There you go. Theeere you go.
ISABEL.   Excuse me. *(Alec, startled, lets the match go out.)*
ALEC.   *(Muttering.)* Fuck.
ISABEL.   Sorry. The thing is … the thing is —
ALEC.   Hi.
ISABEL.   It's — is this some kind of occasion?
ALEC.   Pardon me, I didn't see you there. I didn't realize anyone was …
ISABEL.   You reserved the roof for this occasion.
ALEC.   No. I didn't. Pardon me but at two o'clock in the morning, I honestly didn't think anyone would be …
ISABEL.   Everyone's asleep, you thought.

ALEC. Possibly. Possibly they're asleep, possibly they're not asleep, I don't care honestly. What I care is, they're not on the roof. They're asleep, they're at work, they're drinking chicken soup ... what I care is —
ISABEL. I'm on the roof.
ALEC. Right. Which is why you and I have ... we have a little situation.
ISABEL. I haven't slept in three nights.
ALEC. Right. And my situation is this. I was planning to come up here and eat some Chinese food.
ISABEL. Chinese food.
ALEC. Right. And you were planning, well God knows what you were planning, but since you haven't slept in three nights, allow me to suggest —
ISABEL. What? What's your suggestion? I should go back to bed. I should go back downstairs and climb into bed.
ALEC. Well I don't know. Maybe you were planning to sleep on the roof. But I should tell you I don't think it's a particularly wise idea.
ISABEL. And why is that?
ALEC. Well for one thing, sleepwalking. There's always sleepwalking to think about. And there's another thing. You could get all kinds of weirdos coming up here with all kinds of weirdo ideas. Chinese food, well that could be the least of it, if you know what I mean.
ISABEL. I haven't slept in three nights. I came up here for peace and quiet.
ALEC. There must be other places. Other peaceful, quiet places.
ISABEL. Are you expecting someone?
ALEC. What?
ISABEL. You're expecting someone.
ALEC. Yes. I am, in fact, expecting someone.
ISABEL. Of course.
ALEC. And the truth is, if you must know, the person I'm expecting does not expect to see the two of us. Only one of us is expected.
ISABEL. Who is she?
ALEC. Nobody you know, I'm sure.
ISABEL. Your girlfriend?
ALEC. Right. My girlfriend.
ISABEL. Does she have a name?
ALEC. Yes. Rhonda.
ISABEL. You're right, I don't know any Rhondas.
ALEC. Well that's fine. No reason you should know any Rhondas.

No reason you should be standing here when Rhonda comes up those steps.

ISABEL. You could introduce us.

ALEC. Yes, but this, this was supposed to be a private rendezvous. So I would appreciate it, I really would appreciate it, if you could go and do your not sleeping someplace else.

ISABEL. I was here. I was here first.

ALEC. Yes but —

ISABEL. I made this decision. I unplugged the clock and got out of bed and decided to come to the roof. I don't have the energy to make a different decision.

ALEC. That's ridiculous. That's the most ridiculous thing I've ever heard.

ISABEL. I am not going to sit here, at two o'clock in the morning, and brainstorm other alternatives. I was ... comfortable.

ALEC. Fine. Nobody's asking you to brainstorm. I am simply asking that you consider my situation.

ISABEL. Your situation.

ALEC. Yes. My situation. Maybe tonight's the big night. Maybe I was going to propose.

ISABEL. Were you?

ALEC. Yes. I was going to propose to my girlfriend.

ISABEL. At two o'clock in the morning.

ALEC. Rhonda works nights. She gets off at one.

ISABEL. So where is she?

ALEC. I don't know. She'll be here any minute.

ISABEL. Because if she isn't coming —

ALEC. She's coming. And I'll tell you another thing. If you can't respect that, if you can't respect the fact that my girlfriend is coming up here and I was going to propose, I'll tell you something else. Rhonda has suspicions. She's got all these suspicions. So here I am, ready to propose, and Rhonda's going to come up those steps and see us here, talking like this, wine and candles all around, and she's going to make assumptions. Is that what you want? You want Rhonda to make assumptions.

ISABEL. Listen Mr ...

ALEC. Alec.

ISABEL. Okay, Alec. Listen for a sec, can you? That doesn't make sense. Rhonda knows you're up here, right? So why would she, why would she come up those stairs, and think that you would plan this thing and get her up here, and then accidentally be here with some woman you're seeing. It doesn't make sense.

ALEC. That was an explanation. You want to psychoanalyze, take it apart, fine. You don't like that explanation, I'll give you a different one. Your own explanations haven't exactly been satisfactory. You decided to come to the roof. So what?

ISABEL. I can't explain it.

ALEC. Why not?

ISABEL. I don't know. Because I can't.

ALEC. Try.

ISABEL. Why?

ALEC. I don't know.

ISABEL. Ever had insomnia?

ALEC. Not really.

ISABEL. You do things, when it's two in the morning and you can't sleep, you do things you wouldn't do at any other time. Because you can't stay in bed. It's not an option. Maybe there's this person breathing next to you, not snoring even, just breathing, but it's loud, and you tell yourself, it's not loud, it's like the ocean roaring, and you can sleep next to that. But then all you want to do, is swim into the ocean, and there isn't one. There's just this man next to you, and maybe you had a fight before bed, and maybe you didn't, but there wasn't a wild passionate anything. And he turned off the light, and fell asleep right away, but you have to get out of there. So you take taxis. That's what I do, usually, get in a taxi and ride around and get back before my cash runs out.

ALEC. Taxis.

ISABEL. You asked for an explanation.

ALEC. I asked —

ISABEL. I know, the roof. I'm getting there. The taxi thing gets expensive. And the funny thing is, it was my fiancé who suggested the alternative.

ALEC. Your fiancé?

ISABEL. Yeah. You'd think he'd hate it, waking up alone all the time. And he does, I guess, but maybe he's used to it. I was complaining about the taxi thing, and he said what do you want, and I said privacy, my own space, where do you find that, and he said I don't know, sometimes I go up to the roof. It was a couple of months ago, that he said it. And he's right, you know. It's ... very ...

ALEC. Private?

ISABEL. Yes, private. The other night, it was private. Tonight, well, we're dealing with tonight.

14

ALEC. Are we?

ISABEL. You were going to give me a different explanation.

ALEC. A what?

ISABEL. A different explanation. You said, a few minutes ago, that if I didn't like your explanation, you had a different one.

ALEC. I never said that.

ISABEL. You did. You said those words exactly.

ALEC. I'm wondering something. Do you think, do you think there are many ... couples, in this building? Engaged couples?

ISABEL. Excuse me?

ALEC. Such as yourself. I'm only wondering, if it's a common thing, if there are an infinite variety of ... combinations, such as yourself and ...

ISABEL. Jonathan.

ALEC. Jonathan. And your name, I seem to have forgotten to ... your name is ...

ISABEL. Isabel.

ALEC. Right. Isabel.

ISABEL. You were going to give me an explanation.

ALEC. Right.

ISABEL. I'm beginning to think Rhonda's not coming. I'm beginning to think ...

ALEC. What are you beginning to think?

ISABEL. I have no idea.

ALEC. Here. Take this, take thirty bucks, and grab yourself a cab.

ISABEL. You're giving me thirty dollars?

ALEC. Yes.

ISABEL. What, to leave the roof?

ALEC. Yes. Now.

ISABEL. Now?

ALEC. Preferably now.

ISABEL. I'm not taking your money.

ALEC. I don't want it.

ISABEL. You don't want thirty bucks.

ALEC. Not this thirty bucks. I mean it. Go downstairs and take a cab. Have fun.

ISABEL. You're crazy.

ALEC. Just go. Please.

ISABEL. Okay.

ALEC. Okay?

ISABEL. Okay. *(Isabel crosses to the door, opens it, and steps into the*

15

stairwell. She reemerges a moment later.) Somebody's coming.

ALEC. What?

ISABEL. I can hear her coming up the stairs.

ALEC. Shit. Just a sec. Just give me a sec. *(Alec crosses to the door and begins fiddling with the lock.)*

ISABEL. What are you doing?

ALEC. I'm trying … I am trying to …

ISABEL. You can't lock her out.

ALEC. I am trying to … *(Alec begins opening and closing the door to see if his efforts are successful.)*

ISABEL. You're crazy. *(Alec turns to shut the door, but finds himself face to face with Jonathan.)*

JONATHAN. Isabel. What are you doing up here?

ISABEL. Well that's a funny question. What am I always doing at two o'clock in the morning?

JONATHAN. Riding taxis. I thought you rode taxis.

ISABEL. Sometimes you want a change, something different. You want to go up to the roof and find a total stranger, and argue over contested territory.

JONATHAN. Contested territory.

ALEC. That's right. Contested territory and total strangers. That just about sums it up. I'm Alec Yoshka.

JONATHAN. *(Pause.)* Jonathan Dodd.

ISABEL. And then there were three.

JONATHAN. Excuse me?

ISABEL. It's a nursery rhyme, isn't it? And then there were two, and then there were three. Four, if you count Rhonda.

JONATHAN. Who's Rhonda?

ISABEL. His girlfriend. He's going to propose.

JONATHAN. Are you?

ALEC. Yes.

JONATHAN. Big step.

ALEC. Very big. But when the time is the time …

JONATHAN. I guess.

ISABEL. You guess. You only guess?

JONATHAN. I wasn't … I really wasn't …

ISABEL. What?

JONATHAN. I wasn't talking about us.

ISABEL. Jonathan and I have been engaged nine months. He wasn't, however, talking about us.

JONATHAN. I was talking in the general. People do talk in the general.

ISABEL. Of course they do.

JONATHAN. So, where is she?

ALEC. Who?

JONATHAN. Rhonda?

ALEC. Late. Very late. Which is probably a good thing, seeing as Isabel came up here, and you came up here …

ISABEL. Why did you?

JONATHAN. What?

ISABEL. Come up here.

JONATHAN. I was … looking for you. Why did you come up here?

ISABEL. Fresh air, space, I don't know. *(Pause.)* You never come looking for me.

JONATHAN. Well tonight I did. Maybe I was concerned.

ISABEL. You're all dressed up.

JONATHAN. Well some of us don't like to go about in our pajamas.

ISABEL. Some of us? What is that supposed to mean?

JONATHAN. I felt like getting dressed. That's all I meant.

ISABEL. And all I meant was that it's odd. You don't usually get up and get dressed in your nicest clothes and come looking for me. And how did you know I'd be up here?

ALEC. Excuse me, I'm sorry to interrupt, but seeing as Rhonda is so late, and the two of you have some business to sort out, I'm thinking I'll wait downstairs after all. If Rhonda does show up, if you wouldn't mind explaining the situation …

JONATHAN. Of course.

ALEC. If you wouldn't mind explaining, if she's looking for me later, that I'll be in my apartment for the rest of the night. I should be awake.

JONATHAN. Okay.

ALEC. So then the two of you can have some privacy.

JONATHAN. Okay.

ALEC. To sort out your business.

JONATHAN. *(Pause.)* We don't have any business.

ALEC. Well maybe you do, and maybe you don't.

JONATHAN. We don't.

ALEC. So what you're saying is that there isn't any business. You came up here to find Isabel, and you found her, and you're going to go back downstairs and go to bed, and I'll go downstairs, and if Rhonda never shows up, well that's fine. She and I will have dinner another time, and that will be it. No business of any kind.

JONATHAN. That's what I'm saying.

ALEC. Well I don't know.

JONATHAN. You don't know.

ISABEL. What's happening?

JONATHAN. Nothing. *(Alec crosses to the door to go downstairs and finds it to be locked. Jonathan and Isabel do not see this.)*

ISABEL. Because there's this conversation happening, and I can't really understand it, but it's happening ...

JONATHAN. Nothing's happening.

ALEC. There's just this business ...

JONATHAN. Would you stop saying that, would you stop saying business. What are you saying?

ALEC. Maybe this was supposed to happen. That's what I'm saying. Maybe things are supposed to happen. What is it they say about truth, truth will, what is it, out?

JONATHAN. No.

ALEC. Isabel —

JONATHAN. No.

ALEC. There's somebody I want you to meet. *(Pause.)* This is Rhonda.

ISABEL. Excuse me?

JONATHAN. There's nobody by that name here.

ALEC. Nobody? Are you sure?

JONATHAN. Yes.

ALEC. I beg to differ, Rhonda.

JONATHAN. Don't call me that.

ALEC. Why not?

JONATHAN. Because it's a game, and I don't like games.

ALEC. Oh, it's not a game. This is serious business, Rhonda.

ISABEL. Stop it.

JONATHAN. Don't call me that.

ALEC. Isabel asks me if I'm expecting someone, I say yes, she says what's her name, I say Rhonda. Why don't you tell Isabel who I was expecting.

ISABEL. Oh my God.

ALEC. Exactly. *(To Jonathan.)* Which makes you Rhonda.

JONATHAN. Nothing makes me Rhonda. My name is Jonathan Dodd.

ALEC. Mr. Jonathan Dodd, were you or were you not, on the night of April twenty-sixth —

JONATHAN. No.

ALEC. Were you or were you not planning to join one Alec Yoshka —

ISABEL. Oh my God.

JONATHAN. Why are you doing this?

ALEC. Were you or were you not —

JONATHAN. Why are you doing this?

ALEC. Because it's time. When the time is the time —

JONATHAN. This is crazy. Isabel, you can't listen to him.

ALEC. You think I'm crazy, Isabel? Is that what you think? He got dressed up to look for you, and my girlfriend Rhonda is two hours late, and I'm crazy?

JONATHAN. This is like … an ambush.

ALEC. What do you think, Isabel?

ISABEL. I'm going to be sick.

JONATHAN. You can't do this to me. Isabel — it's an ambush, you can't do this to me.

ISABEL. Do what? I'm not doing anything.

ALEC. It's not an ambush. It's a coincidence. She can't sleep.

ISABEL. Maybe because I'll have nightmares like this.

ALEC. She can't sleep so she came up here. At your suggestion, I might add. Why the fuck, pardon me, but why the fuck would you tell your wife —

ISABEL. Fiancé.

ALEC. Yes, exactly. Why you would tell her to come up to the roof is beyond me.

JONATHAN. I never —

ISABEL. You told me, a few months ago you told me, you said it was …

ALEC. Private.

ISABEL. So I came up here. And you, the two of you came up here because …

ALEC. Because it's what we do. Where we meet.

ISABEL. Jonathan. *(Pause.)* Jonathan.

JONATHAN. … Yes.

ISABEL. Yes?

JONATHAN. Yes.

ISABEL. For how long?

ALEC. Jonathan. I think it's time …

JONATHAN. No.

ALEC. I think it's time —

JONATHAN. No. You keep saying that, but you're wrong. This is not the time. This is some random, ridiculous encounter, on a fucking rooftop. You don't do these things on a rooftop. Most people do not, at two o'clock in the morning, do these things on a rooftop.

ISABEL. Most people.

JONATHAN. Isabel, listen to me. I didn't want it to happen like this.

ISABEL. Right. And most people, they would do this how? Nine o'clock in the morning — coffee and croissants — could you pass the marmalade — and by the way there's this man downstairs —

ALEC. Upstairs.

ISABEL. What?

JONATHAN. He lives upstairs.

ISABEL. Does he? Does he, in fact, live upstairs? And do you, in fact, are you …

ALEC. Yes.

JONATHAN. Yes what. Am I what?

ISABEL. … I don't know.

JONATHAN. What's your question?

ISABEL. I don't know.

ALEC. Good, because he doesn't know the answer.

ISABEL. Just tell me one thing. How long has this been going on?

JONATHAN. About five months.

ISABEL. What were you thinking, this whole time, what were you fucking thinking?

JONATHAN. I don't know.

ALEC. I think she deserves an answer.

JONATHAN. You think you deserve an answer. Would you stop, would you please stop pretending you're worried about Isabel. You don't, I'm sorry, but you don't give a fuck about Isabel.

ISABEL. I feel sick.

ALEC. For your information, for your information Isabel and I were on this roof for a good long time before you graced us with your presence.

JONATHAN. And what … you bonded? The two of you bonded?

ISABEL. Really sick.

JONATHAN. Well that is rich, you know, that's really nice, if you bonded, because, because, you're my two favorite people in the world.

ISABEL. You make me sick. *(Isabel crosses to the edge of the roof, leans over the side and tries to vomit.)*

20

JONATHAN. *(Crossing to Isabel.)* Isabel, baby —

ISABEL. Don't touch me. Don't even think about touching me.

JONATHAN. Okay … okay.

ALEC. *(To Isabel.)* Are you okay?

ISABEL. Don't talk to me. You knew? You knew the whole time? About me.

ALEC. Yes.

ISABEL. He said he was engaged. And what did you say?

ALEC. I don't … remember.

JONATHAN. He laughed.

ISABEL. You laughed?

ALEC. It was … unbelievable.

ISABEL. You laughed at me.

ALEC. No —

ISABEL. I'm not stupid.

ALEC. No —

ISABEL. You think I'm stupid.

ALEC. I never —

ISABEL. Well I'm not. Ever have insomnia?

ALEC. No. We talked about that already.

ISABEL. No. We didn't. We didn't talk about it. Ever go to bed with someone and some nights they won't touch you? Other nights there's something, maybe not passion. A touch. Enough to make excuses, explanations. Not everyone can take your breath away. People have inhibitions, you have to understand that. But then there were those nights I couldn't begin to understand. He wouldn't even meet my eye. Can you imagine that.

ALEC. You wanted to marry this person.

ISABEL. I don't know.

ALEC. It was okay to marry this person.

ISABEL. I don't know. I don't know who it's okay to marry. The guys before, where it was all about the sex. Like they somehow slept through everything else and woke up when we went to bed. The thing is he was there in the morning. Not the morning, that's circumstance, that's nearly everybody. The afternoon. That's the one you marry, the one that gets you through the fucking afternoon.

JONATHAN. Yes, I think that's right.

ISABEL. I'm not talking to you.

JONATHAN. It's the afternoon.

ISABEL. I don't want your opinion, okay? I don't want that. I want —

JONATHAN. What, what do you want?

ALEC. We want the truth.

ISABEL. We. We want?

ALEC. The truth. Something definite.

ISABEL. You want definite? How about marriage? That's supposed to be definite.

ALEC. I wouldn't know.

ISABEL. No, neither would I. I've got to get out of here. *(Isabel rushes to the door and struggles to open it, but it is locked.)* Fuck. Alec, what did you do, what the fuck did you do to the door?

ALEC. I was trying to —

ISABEL. Yeah, well it's locked. You fucking locked it.

JONATHAN. So we're stuck. What you're saying is we're stuck.

ALEC. I'm sorry. I didn't realize …

JONATHAN. We'll get down. There are ways … we'll get down. *(Jonathan crosses to the door and struggles with the lock.)*

ALEC. Now this I'd like to see. Jonathan finding a way out. Sorry, down, not out. A way down.

JONATHAN. Thank you. We're stuck on the fucking roof, and you're playing word games. Thanks so much, very helpful.

ALEC. Couldn't resist.

JONATHAN. We will get off this roof.

ALEC. Ever consider jumping?

ISABEL. Yes.

ALEC. Please don't. You gonna be okay?

ISABEL. What do you think?

JONATHAN. Do you need some water?

ISABEL. No.

ALEC. What kind of question is that? Do we have any water? Do you see any water to be had?

JONATHAN. I was trying to help.

ALEC. Yeah, keep trying.

JONATHAN. Where's your cell phone?

ALEC. My what?

JONATHAN. Your cell phone that you bring everywhere, like you're some Wall Street kid. For once it could serve a purpose.

ALEC. … I left it downstairs.

ISABEL. You what?

ALEC. Left it downstairs. My cell phone. *(Isabel gets up and crosses to the chair over which Alec's jacket is draped.)*

JONATHAN. Of course.

ALEC. Isabel. What are you doing?

ISABEL. *(Taking the jacket.)* Maybe I'm cold. Maybe I'm going to throw up all over your jacket. *(Isabel pulls the cell phone out of the jacket pocket.)* Maybe I'm looking for this. You ordered the fucking Chinese food, remember?

JONATHAN. You said it was downstairs.

ALEC. I forgot.

JONATHAN. You forgot?

ALEC. I was confused. This whole night has been so crazy …

JONATHAN. You had, in your jacket pocket, the one thing that could get us off this roof, and you forgot.

ALEC. Isabel was kind enough to remind me. Who are you going to call?

ISABEL. That's the thing. I don't know.

ALEC. Two-thirty in the morning.

ISABEL. I have a friend … she's in Brooklyn, but she could call somebody. *(Isabel dials and waits.)* Hi Doris, it's Isabel. Either you're asleep, or you're out dancing or something. But if you're there, would you please WAKE UP. It's a bit of a crisis. So please WAKE UP and PICK UP THE PHONE. WAKE UP, DORIS. *(Pause.)* Okay? I guess you're not there. Okay. Bye. *(Isabel hangs up the phone.)*

ALEC. I know somebody. He's perfect. Lives just down the block. *(Alec holds out his hand.)* Here. *(Isabel hands Alec the phone. Alec takes it and begins to dial. He stops dialing and slides open the battery compartment. Alec takes the batteries out of the phone and pockets them. He holds out the phone to Isabel.)* Here.

ISABEL. What are you doing?

ALEC. He's not home.

JONATHAN. You didn't even dial.

ALEC. He's not home. Here.

ISABEL. *(Taking the phone.)* You have the battery pack.

ALEC. True.

ISABEL. What are you doing?

ALEC. Things happen for a reason. People get stuck for a reason.

JONATHAN. We're not stuck.

ALEC. Everyone's always running away. Until one day they get stuck. They have to face things.

JONATHAN. We're not stuck. Just give us the batteries.

ALEC. Of course. Just give us some answers.

JONATHAN. Give me the fucking batteries.

ALEC. No. *(Jonathan lunges for the batteries, the two men struggle violently, nearing the edge of the roof. Jonathan has lost control; Alec attempts to defend himself. Isabel watches, attempting to stop them.)*
ISABEL. Stop it — please — what are you doing? ... STOP IT! I said — JONATHAN! *(Isabel comes between them.)* Stop it. Both of you. We're twelve stories up.
JONATHAN. *(To Alec.)* What is it you want? What do you fucking want?
ALEC. I want you to figure it out. You're in the same goddamn fog you were the night we met. You do remember that night?
JONATHAN. Yes. Of course.
ALEC. Where were we?
JONATHAN. Oscar's. Across the street.
ALEC. Why did you go in there?
JONATHAN. I had an argument with Isabel. I wanted to sit somewhere and think things through.
ALEC. It's a gay bar. Oscar's for God's sake.
JONATHAN. I wanted a beer.
ALEC. Yes, but —
JONATHAN. It's across the street.
ALEC. Fine. Whatever.
JONATHAN. I was minding my own business.
ALEC. Yes. You were. And I checked you out, but I saw it right away.
JONATHAN. Saw what?
ALEC. That you were so far beyond confused that you came out the other side with some ridiculous kind of clarity. Sitting there in your suit, telling me about your life, about law school, interviewing at all these firms. About your girlfriend. All these words, and all I could think was, this man needs something, he needs help.
JONATHAN. Help?
ALEC. Yes.
JONATHAN. Fuck that. No, no thank you. What was it, some kind of power trip for you, I needed your help?
ALEC. No, it wasn't that. I felt for you. Because I've been there too, knowing things you can't let yourself know —
JONATHAN. Alec —
ALEC. — constructing this whole other life, I know that, how hard it is. But then, the first time you meet somebody —
JONATHAN. Alec —

24

ALEC. You meet somebody, and this thing that's so hard in the abstract is suddenly so right. I know that too. How you meet somebody, and for the first time —

JONATHAN. Alec —

ALEC. It's ... it's ...

JONATHAN. You weren't the first time.

ALEC. What?

JONATHAN. There was —

ALEC. What are you talking about?

JONATHAN. This guy. Before.

ISABEL. When?

ALEC. Why didn't you tell me?

ISABEL. Jonathan? ... When?

JONATHAN. Four years ago. His name was Pete. We met in London, on Goodge Street. He used to say that word over and over, to make me laugh. He would whisper it sometimes, first thing in the morning. Before I even opened my eyes. Goodge.

ISABEL. What happened?

JONATHAN. He left me. For somebody else, this other guy. And nobody knew, it was this big secret and I couldn't talk to anybody back here, and I came home and thought maybe I imagined the whole thing. Maybe it never happened.

ALEC. You never told me.

JONATHAN. Maybe it never happened.

ALEC. Bullshit.

JONATHAN. After he left, I used to wake up to that word, like somebody had whispered it. But nobody was there. And one morning, I thought I can't do this, if it's going to feel like this ever again I can't do it.

ISABEL. And then what, you went back to women.

JONATHAN. When I met you, it was something, it was, you were —

ALEC. Safe?

JONATHAN. A friend. That's what I needed. Like you said, if it gets you through the afternoon.

ALEC. What are you talking about? Both of you, going on about the afternoon. Wake up, it's called fear, no matter what time it is.

JONATHAN. I said I needed a friend.

ALEC. Fine. Get yourself a friend. Marry her. Plan an afternoon wedding. How about three o'clock? Let's finalize this thing right now. I think you should propose, just to clarify things. Just in case there's been any confusion.

JONATHAN. What are you talking about?

ALEC. I think you should propose to Isabel.

JONATHAN. No.

ALEC. *(Demonstrating.)* Isabel, will you marry me?

ISABEL. Stop it.

ALEC. Come on, just so we know where we stand. *(To Jonathan.)* Go ahead, get on one knee. *(Alec pushes Jonathan onto his knees.)*

ISABEL. Stop it. We're not — nobody's getting married.

ALEC. I just want to make sure.

JONATHAN. I told you already —

ALEC. I just want to know what you want. Who you want. Isabel, will you … will you —

JONATHAN. *(Breaking away.)* I won't do this.

ALEC. You can't do it. You can't fucking say it. Marry me. Marry me, Isabel. On your knees. That's how it's done, isn't it? *(Alec pushes Jonathan on to his knees again, harder this time.)*

ISABEL. Please. Don't.

ALEC. On your fucking knees. *(Jonathan breaks away and crosses to the edge of the roof to get away from Alec, trying to catch his breath. Alec moves back, watching. Alec turns to look at Isabel and then slowly crosses to Jonathan. Jonathan stares at Alec, then suddenly goes to embrace him. Holding Jonathan.)* You never told me, about that guy. This whole time, you were lying to both of us.

ISABEL. *(To Alec.)* Welcome to the roof. It's a scary place. *(Isabel crosses to a different corner of the roof, too close to the edge.)*

JONATHAN. *(Noticing Isabel.)* Isabel, what are you doing?

ISABEL. Were you ever scared of heights? None of us.

JONATHAN. Please, come away from the edge.

ISABEL. Most people are terrified. They call it vertigo.

JONATHAN. Alec, the batteries. Now, before something happens.

ALEC. She'll be all right.

JONATHAN. How do you know?

ALEC. Because she's leaving you.

ISABEL. Vertigo. I'm looking. At all the windows. I just want … I just want to look.

JONATHAN. What about you?

ALEC. Me.

JONATHAN. Are you leaving me? *(Alec stares at Jonathan, but does not answer. He crosses to Isabel and holds out the batteries.)*

ALEC. Here. Call somebody. *(Isabel replaces the batteries and dials.)*

ISABEL. Yes, I'm on the roof, of my building. Three of us. And we can't, right now, get down. Yes. Please. Thanks. Yes. *(Isabel waits. Alec and Jonathan watch her. The lights fade slowly to black. Curtain.)*

End of Play

PROPERTY LIST

Headphones, sweatshirt (ISABEL)
Cell phone (ALEC, ISABEL)
Bottle of wine, two glasses, candles, matches (ALEC)

WATERBORN
by Edith L. Freni

CHARACTERS

MARK, mid-30s/early 40s. Tall, thin, baby-faced, an administrative peon. As earnest as they come, a little deluded and trying desperately to make the best of a bad situation.

LESLIE, early/mid-30s. Small, brassy, foul-mouthed, about four months pregnant. A career chef, she definitely wears the pants in this family. Guilt-ridden but hiding it well, intent upon getting her husband to take a stand for once.

SETTING

An alternative birthing center somewhere in NYC.

WATERBORN

*Mark and Leslie stand next to a large birthing pool. It is empty.
There is a rocking chair upstage. To its side, a small mahogany
table with lamp that glows soft white light. He, a thin, spindly
man with a real baby face, wears a sports coat and glasses, seems
happy. She, a rather small, rough-and-tumble-looking woman
in clogs and sweatpants, is vaguely pregnant, probably around
four months. After a brief pause:*

LESLIE. So you're saying I can't have drugs?
MARK. You wouldn't need them.
LESLIE. Right. And you would be where?
MARK. In there with you.
LESLIE. Why?!?
MARK. For support.
LESLIE. Are you naked too?
MARK. If you want me to be.
LESLIE. *(Moderately skeeved out.)* Um ... yeah, not so much.
MARK. Okay. That's ... fine too. Whatever makes you comfort-
able. That's all that really matters.
LESLIE. Is it?
MARK. Of course. This is *your* birthing experience. The aim is to
make you happy, to keep things as simple as possible.
LESLIE. Simple?
MARK. Yes! Quick and easy. Goldenrod said —
LESLIE. — I'm sorry, *Goldenrod?*
MARK. The midwife. That was her name, were you paying atten-
tion?
LESLIE. No. I wasn't. Goldenrod said what now?
MARK. Leslie, I swear, sometimes —
LESLIE. — Just tell me what she said.
MARK. She said that some people are in and outta here in like an
hour flat. Those Hasidic women she was talking about. They just

31

drop and go.

LESLIE. Well that's great for Jews, but what about us?

MARK. Huh. I don't think it really makes a difference.

LESLIE. What does the Church think about water births?

MARK. *(All aglow.)* You know, I'd never even thought to ask. I'll run it by Father Rufus. I'm sure he'd be happy to check.

LESLIE. Mark?

MARK. Yes, dear?

LESLIE. It was a joke. I couldn't give two steaming shits what they think.

MARK. No. Of course you couldn't. I should have known you were kidding. I'm sorry. However —

LESLIE. — No! No "However," however my ass. This is not an issue you need to discuss with him.

MARK. But —

LESLIE. — It was a joke, Mark! I don't think I need to make myself any clearer on this but if I do, you let me know, and I will, okay?

MARK. You don't. You're right. This is not about him.

LESLIE. It's about me. *My* birthing experience. Not the priest's.

MARK. *(Beat.)* Okay then. So. What do you think? *(She takes a moment. Looks around.)*

LESLIE. I dunno. It's a hot tub. I'm supposed to get excited about a fuckin' Jacuzzi.

MARK. This is a birthing pool, Les, not a hot tub.

LESLIE. Looks like the tub from our suite at Lavajolla.

MARK. It is a POOL for BIRTHING! *(She steadies herself, fighting off a wave of nausea.)*

LESLIE. Oh God, I think I'm going to vomit.

MARK. *(Quickly.)* Please don't do it in the pool!

LESLIE. I wouldn't DO IT in the pool, what do you think I am, some kind of animal?!

MARK. Leslie —

LESLIE. — No, don't take it back now, you can't just say "Leslie" and take it back. You said it, I'm an animal.

MARK. I didn't say animal —

LESLIE. — And you know, so what? So what if I vomit in the pool? Is puke really that much worse than afterbirth?

MARK. What's so bad about afterbirth?

LESLIE. EVERYTHING! Birth is vile, Mark. Messy, complicated. Whether it's in a hospital bed or a pool.

MARK. It's more soothing in the pool.

LESLIE. Won't be for me. I hate water.

MARK. Since when?!?

LESLIE. How soon we forget. Jones Beach. July 4th. Two years ago.

MARK. You got caught in a riptide!

LESLIE. Yeah? And?

MARK. And you got yourself out of it.

LESLIE. I could have very easily drowned!

MARK. You're not gonna drown in here, the whole thing is one big shallow end!

LESLIE. Hundreds of children drown in toilets every year.

MARK. Yeah, but you know your head from your asshole.

LESLIE. That's the nicest thing you've ever said to me.

MARK. Les, come on, come here for a sec, all right? I want you to focus, okay? Take a deep breath, close your eyes ...

LESLIE. Mark, geez, I don't wanna —

MARK. — PLEASE CLOSE YOUR EYES, LESLIE! Just ... for a second. *(She does so. He glows. Unlike a man.)* Close your eyes and try to feel the warm water surrounding you, holding you, supporting you. Think about how life-affirming, how beautiful and special and —

LESLIE. — Okay, you have got to stop trying to make it sound so magical.

MARK. But it is!

LESLIE. No it's not, see, because *magic* is pulling rabbits out of hats and making decks of cards appear out of thin air which ... would be great in the case of babies but alas it is not magic that causes perfectly normal women to grunt and scream and BLEED PROFUSELY and totally lose bowel control before forcing something the size of a rabbit out of something the size of a deck of cards. THAT is just "the way it is" and THAT does not sound like so much fun to me, in fact, it's always sounded like a rather humiliating way to spend six to twenty-four hours. So, you'll forgive me, but if I'm gonna have to go through all that shit, I don't want to be conscious of its happening. I don't want to *feel* it or *experience* it — I'll tell you what I want — I want a hospital gown, a bed and strong painkillers. I want a *doctor*, a couple nurses maybe — all female by the way — and I want you in the waiting room, pacing back and forth with a cigar in your shirt pocket just like my father did. No camcorders pointed at my fucking cunt, no sweat-drenched hair stroking, I-love-you-so-much-honeys. No weepy

33

moments after it's all over and certainly no visitors while I recoup. Sorry but this chick, not into it. Blame my mother if you wanna blame someone but don't look at me 'cause you knew I was this way when we got married. *(He looks at her funny. A moment.)*

MARK. I don't think I did know.

LESLIE. We had this conversation the night you proposed.

MARK. Well our situation has changed, hasn't it? The dynamics of our relationship have, how shall I say, *shifted* just a wee bit? Wouldn't you agree?

LESLIE. Yes I *would* agree that's what I'm saying, I feel like —

MARK. — Now it's totally understandable that you're a little freaked out but —

LESLIE. PLEASE don't cut me off —

MARK. *(Overlapping.)* I've done quite a bit of research on this birthing stuff. Trying to find the best way for *you* to deliver —

LESLIE.	MARK.
— listen to me and I'll tell you what I want, I don't want to SCREAM about — Please be quiet, oh you don't know the half of it sweetheart!	See and I'm doing all this because somebody has to and for one reason or another this, you don't seem to give a shit and I know you hate hospitals so —

LESLIE. I never said I hated hospitals.

MARK. You did the last time I asked you to visit me at work.

LESLIE. That's 'cause I didn't want to come visit you! Hello?!?

MARK. Why not?

LESLIE. Like I really want to watch you rubber-stamp and file shit all day long.

MARK. You think I'd make you just sit there? Twiddling your thumbs? I could introduce you around. Prove to everyone that I *do actually have a wife*. We could have a picnic.

LESLIE. A picnic in that tiny gray hole you call an office. Sounds wonderful.

MARK. I meant on the grounds. They're quite lovely.

LESLIE. It's not even a real hospital.

MARK. I'm only saying I wouldn't mind seeing you more often.

LESLIE. Then you come visit me at fucking work! *(Dead silence. A beat. He turns away. Goes to the pool. When they finally begin speaking to each other, they do so slowly and with caution.)* You know I'm long gone by the time he gets into that kitchen.

MARK. I'm sure you cross paths on the rare occasion.

34

LESLIE. I do my best to avoid the rare occasion.

MARK. No you don't.

LESLIE. I don't?

MARK. Doing your best would have meant quitting.

LESLIE. I'm sorry. I didn't know that you wanted me to quit.

MARK. Well ... maybe I did.

LESLIE. Then why didn't you ask me to? *(Beat. He walks away from her. She follows him.)* Why didn't you TELL me that's what you wanted? *(He says nothing.)* Answer the fucking question please!

MARK. Why would I ask you to quit when I know how happy that job makes you? Why? When I live and breathe for your happiness? Huh? I didn't think I'd need you to quit. I figured I could just deal.

LESLIE. But you can't.

MARK. Yes I can.

LESLIE. *(At pool.)* Mark, look at this shit. This is you dealing? We are not these people.

MARK. We could be.

LESLIE. I don't think so.

MARK. FINE then no pool. I got it. Let's go.

LESLIE. Where? What's next? Bowling alley? Tennis court?

MARK. Please don't make jokes, Leslie.

LESLIE. Or wait! I got an even better idea! How 'bout I have him in the kitchen?

MARK. You're funny.

LESLIE. Since this is all about *my* comfort and *my* happiness, I'll just have him on the line. Squat right over the slop sink and Bardo can wash him off like a dinner plate.

MARK. *(Approaching her.)* You are a sicko.

LESLIE. And you have no sense of humor.

MARK. That's not funny. At all.

LESLIE. Pat would have laughed. He would have found it funny.

MARK. Pat has no moral compass.

LESLIE. But he can sure make babies.

MARK. The hospital then.

LESLIE. I didn't SAY I wanted the hospital!

MARK. Well you have to have it somewhere!

LESLIE. Are you telling me what to do?

MARK. No, of course I'm —

LESLIE. — 'Cause it kinda sounded like maybe you were!

LESLIE. Jesus give me strength, if you don't cooperate —

MARK. — What?!? Oh what?!? What's gonna happen? You gonna put your foot down? PLEASE! Put your foot down. I've been begging for it for nearly a decade. *(He hesitates.)*

MARK. I'm not your father.

LESLIE. No you're not. My father could make a decision.

MARK. It's your baby you decide.

LESLIE. Good puppy.

MARK. Don't do that.

LESLIE. Then take a stand for once.

MARK. Okay, have the baby, in the water.

LESLIE. Why?

MARK. Because I think it would be nice for you. I think it would be a great personal growth experience.

LESLIE. Now I need to grow?

MARK. Look, I'm *really* getting sick of fighting with you about this.

LESLIE. What are you talking about?!? Are you — you gotta be married to somebody else or something and maybe you've been fighting with the other wife but you sure as hell haven't been fighting with me!

MARK. Whaddaya, *want* to fight with me?

LESLIE. All I want is to get the truth outta you.

MARK. What *truth*? The truth about what?

LESLIE. Why we're here. Why are we HERE?!?

MARK. We're here to see the pool!

LESLIE. I don't mean here, I mean why are *we* HERE?!?

MARK. I'm sorry, I just don't understand what you're asking.

LESLIE. What are you attempting?

MARK. Attempting?

LESLIE. Your intentions, Mark and don't play dumb with me!

MARK. My inten ... My *intention*, my ONE DESIRE, has been, is now, and will always be to protect our family against those external forces that seek to destroy us morally, physically and spiritually from the inside out. That is my intention.

LESLIE. *(Beat.)* Ah. That. *(Long pause. She stares him down.)* Extended Mass, huh?

MARK. What?

LESLIE. Staying late to dish out macaroni salad and meatballs. Working the coffee pot. HA! You're such a good boy.

MARK. Forgive me for feeling the need to give a little back.

LESLIE. Now I understand why you were so happy I had to pick up brunch last weekend.

MARK. You never come anyway.

LESLIE. Christmas and Easter.

MARK. That's nothing.

LESLIE. It's about all I can stomach. *(Beat.)* So what did he say?

MARK. Who?

LESLIE. Big Daddy Rufus.

MARK. Don't call him that.

LESLIE. How does he feel about this alternative nonsense?

MARK. I told you, I haven't discussed it with him.

LESLIE. Then what have you discussed?

MARK. That's private, Leslie.

LESLIE. Oh FUCK YOU! I cheat, I spill my GUTS to you. You betray me and it's private?

MARK. I'm sorry?! Are you kidding?

LESLIE. Talking to *him* about THIS is a betrayal!

MARK. You can't just tell a person a thing like what you told me and expect him not to go looking for a little guidance.

LESLIE. You want guidance? You're surrounded by shrinks five days a week!

MARK. I didn't want to see a shrink.

LESLIE. Why not?

MARK. Because I'm not confused about how I feel or why I feel, I'm confused about what I need to do in order not to feel this way anymore.

LESLIE. And therein lies the beauty of the Catholic Church.

MARK. Think what you want to think.

LESLIE. Thanks, I will. *(Beat.)* I don't want you talking to him about this anymore.

MARK. Leslie, that is completely unfair!

LESLIE. NO MORE, Mark! NO MORE! *(Long pause. He looks down and away from her.)*

MARK. We only ever talked about forgiveness.

LESLIE. And have you forgiven me?

MARK. Yes.

LESLIE. Just like that?

MARK. Yes.

LESLIE. It's all right if you haven't.

MARK. But I have. *(Beat.)* So when I say I want to see you more, I mean it. When I suggest something like the pool, I'm only doing so because I think it'll make things nicer for you. So if you don't want to do this here, then fine. We'll figure something else out. Just tell me so we can be done with it.

LESLIE. If I make a decision will you stand by me?

MARK. You know I will.

LESLIE. And if I REALLY don't like this idea I can tell you and we can just forget about it?

MARK. Of course.

LESLIE. And I get FINAL say in where I have this child?

MARK. Yes.

LESLIE. Then I pick *nowhere*, Mark. I pick "nowhere" to have this baby because I don't *want* to have this baby.

MARK. But ... but you have to. Have it.

LESLIE. No I don't.

MARK. You agreed.

LESLIE. Well I changed my mind.

MARK. Why?

LESLIE. Because you said you needed this in order to move on —

MARK. — It was true, what I said.

LESLIE. But we haven't moved anywhere!

MARK. It's been what, two months? Give it some time.

LESLIE. Things aren't gonna get any better.

MARK. They will if we try, if we want them to.

LESLIE. It's not enough to just want it.

MARK. Why are you doing this to me?

LESLIE. Why are *you* doing this to *me*?

MARK. I'm not doing anything to you!

LESLIE. I am a catastrophe! I don't even feel like I'm living in my own body anymore. I can't sleep, I can't breath, I'm anxious all the time. *(He grabs her by the shoulders and pushes her to the edge of the pool.)*

MARK. You are not going to get rid of this baby.

LESLIE. Okay, then so just get rid of me, would you?!? Put me out of my misery because THAT'S WHAT THIS IS! *(Pause. He shakes with anger and frustration, fear and resentment.)* DO IT! Do something, would you?!? Just fucking hit me or kick me or DROWN ME. I don't care but just DO SOMETHING! *(Beat. He quakes, thinking. His mind races. Finally, he kisses her violently, a little awkwardly, throwing his body into hers. This is terribly unexpected and she does not reciprocate, tries to get away. He pulls at her shirt, trying to get it off.)* Mark! Stop it. What the hell are you doing?!? *(He doesn't answer, keeps at her, moving down her body, shoving his face between her breasts, into her stomach, groin. She doesn't quite know what to make of this but, suffice it to say, she is not enjoying it; pulling away, pushing him. This altercation should never come off as overly malicious on his part but more bizarre and awkward, nearly comical.)* Get off of me. Mark! STOP IT.

MARK. You wanted me to do something, well I'm doing it!

LESLIE. Not this. Goddamnit! GET THE FUCK OFF ME! *(Finally, she manages to pull away, kneeing him in the face as she does so. His glasses fly off, he is on his hands and knees trying to find them, trying to collect himself, hiding his face from her view.)* Jesus Christ, I'm sorry. *(He removes a tissue from his pocket, puts it to his nose, tilts his head back.)* I'm SORRY. It was an accident. Would you look at me, please? *(Pause.)* Mark —

MARK. *(Turning to her/roaring.)* WHAT?! *(She jumps a bit. Beat. They are silent. His nose is bloody.)* I'm LOOKING! So? What? Yeah, I see you. I see how unhappy you are. You think I'm trying to punish you but I'm not.

LESLIE. Then WHAT are you doing? *(Pause. He looks up at her.)*

MARK. Did you know, Leslie that I see him everywhere I go? Every time I try to get close to you, there he is. I know you see him too. He's standing right between us. *(Beat.)* And I know you want to be with him.

LESLIE. I don't though. Mark, I swear to you I don't.

MARK. Well, then I want you to be with him. I want to be him, I wanna be with — I just wanna BE HIM for you. But I can't be. No matter how hard I try. No matter what I do, what I am, is never gonna be what you want. I don't know how to make you happy anymore. So what the fuck, huh?!? Did I ever — did I ever make you happy? Did you ever love me?

LESLIE. Of course I did —

MARK. — THEN WHY WOULD YOU DO THIS?! WHY? Tell me.

LESLIE. I don't know.

MARK. FUCK THAT! We're talking now! You wanted to talk, well we're talking. So talk. *(Beat.)* TALK you selfish bitch, get it out now.

LESLIE. It wasn't about anything other than just WANTING each other. That was it. Nothing else. Mark, I know it was stupid, I know it was a mistake —

MARK. — Damned right it was a mistake! It was a mistake that RUINED EVERYTHING! You. Are. Everything to me. And I am NOTHING in your eyes. You just wanted him! Bullshit. You just

DIDN'T WANT me. It could have been anyone so long as it wasn't
ME. You didn't even love me enough in that moment to protect
yourself, to protect us from HIM you ... filthy ... SLUT. You let
him put his dick in you and you won't even let me near enough to
hold your hand. You let him fuck you, I try to kiss you and ... what's
wrong with me Leslie? Am I so horrible? Am I so disgusting to you?
(She says nothing. He collapses into the rocking chair.) I don't know anything. What's right or wrong, what's truth ... I'm so confused about
what I need to do to just *exist* in this world. I want our life to be what
it was when we met. Simple. Not so messy, not so complicated. I
don't think that's too much to ask for. *(Beat.)* I go to Rufus 'cause I
think he's got answers for me. But all he has to say is, "Forgive.
Forget. Move on." How? Have the baby. Because having the baby
means forgiveness. I thought it was gonna be that easy.
LESLIE. But it's not.
MARK. I just figured ... if you could have the baby in the water,
then all of this would be washed away. *(Long pause. Leslie walks to
the pool. She takes a moment to examine it.)*
LESLIE. Huh. You know, it kinda looks *exactly* like the tub from
Lavajolla. *(A moment. He smiles, shyly, slightly embarrassed maybe,
then he looks up at her.)*
MARK. I can't believe you actually remember what that tub
looked like.
LESLIE. No girl forgets her honeymoon, honey. *(She gets in.
Reclines. Looks straight out.)*
MARK. Like Lavajolla. *(After a brief pause, he joins her in the pool.
They gaze at one another. Beat.)*
LESLIE. Yeah. Just like Lavajolla. *(Lights fade.)*

End of Play

PROPERTY LIST

Tissue (MARK)

CHARLIE BLAKE'S BOAT

by Graeme Gillis

CHARACTERS

HELEN

CHARLIE

PLACE

Mahone Bay, a small maritime town.

TIME

The present.
Late August.

CHARLIE BLAKE'S BOAT

Lights up on the wharf. It is made of logs and iron twine, and stretches the length of the stage. This is Mahone Bay, a small maritime town, present day in late August. Charlie Blake sits alone, his legs dangling. He is whittling something out of a big block of wood with a Swiss Army knife. A line of unopened champagne bottles sits beside him. Behind him sits his boat. You can hear it bumping up against the wharf and the water lapping in the early morning quiet. In the distance are happy voices, stragglers at the nearby party. It is not yet dawn. A homemade banner stretches over part of the wharf. It reads "Bonne Voyagee Charlie Blake." There is also a church banner, purple like for Easter or Advent, that reads "God Bless Charlie Blake's Boat." Charlie kills the last of his bottle. He pops another open, and the cork sails into the air. From off-stage we hear Helen singing "Farewell To Nova Scotia."

HELEN. "Farewell to Nova Scotia, the sea-bound coast / Let your mountains dark and dreary be / But when I am far away on the briny ocean toss'd / Will you ever heave a sigh or a wish for me?" *(Enter Helen. She sees the church banner. When she speaks Charlie knows her right away.)* "God Bless Charlie Blake's Boat."
CHARLIE. Ahh, Jesus.
HELEN. "God bless him and keep him from the dangers of the sea."
CHARLIE. Helen Lucille McNeil.
HELEN. "And God do not forsake this Godforsaken tub of a boat, or this Godforsaken tub of a man. Amen."
CHARLIE. Welcome home Helen.
HELEN. Thanks.
CHARLIE. Been a long time.
HELEN. It has. *(They begin to shake hands, then laugh and begin to hug, then think better of it and shake hands.)*
CHARLIE. You look like about a million bucks.

HELEN. And you look like about seventy-five cents. It's good to see you.

CHARLIE. It is?

HELEN. Yeah, I'm a little surprised myself. *(They do the hand-shake-or-hug thing again, but this time it ends in a hug. This leads to more discomfort. They let go.)* They're praying for you up at the party, you know. Father Bernie's doing his best but Alec's got his pants on his head and Sheilagh's hanging off the roof. By her ankles. Till Alec pays attention to her she says. It's that time of night. Anyway you should see it. You might not see it for a while.

CHARLIE. So what brings you back this way?

HELEN. Heard about the party, you know? Hate to miss a party. *(Reads.)* "Bonne voyagee, Charlie Blake." *(She laughs and shakes her head.)* Well. Bonne voyagee. *(She kills the last of her bottle.)* Farewell to Nova Scotia.

CHARLIE. And you came all this way for that?

HELEN. Ah, it was just a plane and a bus.

CHARLIE. Ah yes, the bus from Bullshit City.

HELEN. Come on Charlie.

CHARLIE. Sorry, I'm sorry. How are things? How are things in Bullshit City?

HELEN. Good.

CHARLIE. Great.

HELEN. Good. Yeah. Onward and upward. All the time.

CHARLIE. Well that's great.

HELEN. So. What're you whittling there?

CHARLIE. It's a figurehead. For the stem. For the boat.

HELEN. What's it supposed to be?

CHARLIE. Speck.

HELEN. Speck?

CHARLIE. My uncle Speck.

HELEN. Oh. Oh right.

CHARLIE. It's a work in progress.

HELEN. I can see that.

CHARLIE. Yeah well I'm a bit behind so you'll have to excuse me. Got to be done by morning. Last thing before I'm off.

HELEN. To Scotland.

CHARLIE. That's right. Make my mother happy.

HELEN. I've seen your mother up at the party, she's beside herself.

CHARLIE. She's pleased to have the house to herself, I think.

HELEN. So what's in Scotland?

CHARLIE. Ah I don't know. Bagpipes I guess. Kilts. Heroin.

HELEN. Right.

CHARLIE. My mother was there once, we've got family over there. Mum says it's more beautiful than Ireland, and they're not as smug as the Irish are either. No "luck of the Scottish" bullshit or anything, you know. I just want to see it. I want to see where I come from.

HELEN. You come from here.

CHARLIE. Well that's not ... quite enough. For me.

HELEN. You'd like a little more glam, eh? Little more flash.

CHARLIE. No man, glam and flash, that's your thing.

HELEN. Is it.

CHARLIE. That's what I hear.

HELEN. Well you can say you're from wherever you want. You can make it all up. But you belong here.

CHARLIE. Well I think I'd like to decide. Where I belong. I'd like a say. Instead of someone telling me.

HELEN. So Scotland then.

CHARLIE. For a start. *(Pops new cork, it sails overhead.)* So how're you fitting in up there?

HELEN. Just fine, thanks.

CHARLIE. Just asking is all. Old Mahone Bay you know, the old gang — gone three years and all, it can be a bit awkward.

HELEN. No, I'm fine. They're fine. It's great to see everybody.

CHARLIE. Well good.

HELEN. Can't wait, can you?

CHARLIE. Well you know how that feels, right? You couldn't wait, right? To be off? I remember that much.

HELEN. *(Holds her tongue, takes a swig.)* So let me ask you something Charlie, how do you figure on making it to Maine, let alone Scotland, in this —

CHARLIE. Careful.

HELEN. What?

CHARLIE. Well — just don't talk bad about her.

HELEN. I wasn't going to say anything bad. In this ... contraption.

CHARLIE. There's just, a lot of my life in that contraption is all.

HELEN. Right.

CHARLIE. A long time.

HELEN. Yeah.

CHARLIE. And anyway I'm going to Australia first. Then Scotland.

HELEN. But how will you get there?

CHARLIE. Same way you get anywhere from Australia. You go up.

HELEN. But how —

CHARLIE. Port to port, all right, Helen? Port to port. From here to Maine, and from Maine right on down the seaboard. Till I hit the Bahamas. Then get a tow across to Australia and from there just head up to Scotland. Port to port. Down one side and up the other side. It's a circumnavigation, you get it? An old-fashioned, Magellan-style, swabby, scurvy circumnavigation. And if you ever read your own mail you'd know all this. Goddamnit!

HELEN. What?

CHARLIE. I got a splinter.

HELEN. Well here, come here.

CHARLIE. *(Tries to suck his own splinter.)* No, I'm fine.

HELEN. Gimme.

CHARLIE. Look will you get out of it and let me handle this please?

HELEN. How long?

CHARLIE. What — ow! Fuck! — what?

HELEN. How LONG. The whole trip, how long?

CHARLIE. Arrgh, three Goddamn years.

HELEN. You're gonna spend three years in that —

CHARLIE. Will you quit calling her names? It's not a contraption and it's not a tub either, see? It's a boat. All right? It's a BOAT. It's a ship.

HELEN. Well what kinda ship is that?

CHARLIE. It's a schooner.

HELEN. That's not a schooner.

CHARLIE. It is.

HELEN. It's too small to be a schooner.

CHARLIE. *(Angrily whittles.)* It's a pinky schooner. And if you knew anything about anything, you'd know that.

HELEN. What're you calling it then? Pinky?

CHARLIE. No. It's really more of a sloop than a schooner anyway. It's based off the old sloops from the 1800s —

HELEN. So then Sloopy.

CHARLIE. No. No. Not Pinky. Not Sloopy. Jesus — fuck! — ow.

HELEN. Here. *(Takes his hand.)* Now don't look. So what're you going to call it then. If not Pinky or Sloopy. *(Helen moves to suck splinter out. It's pretty sexy. Charlie looks in spite of himself.)*

CHARLIE. I … don't know.

HELEN. I told you not to look. *(Spits splinter out.)* There.

CHARLIE. You didn't have to do that.

HELEN. No. So?

CHARLIE. You didn't have to come back here either.

HELEN. Well. God bless ya. *(Chucks him on the shoulder or chin.)* Captain Blake. And God bless your boat. *(He says nothing, so she finishes bottle.)* Aren't you supposed to break one of these over the side? *(Grabs bottle, brings it to ship's bow.)* I christen this contraption, Pinky.

CHARLIE. Her name's not Pinky.

HELEN. Pinky Contraption, the Brave Little Schooner.

CHARLIE. Don't do it on the wood.

HELEN. You said it was all wood.

CHARLIE. See. The bow plate's iron, hit the bow plate.

HELEN. Your letter said all wood.

CHARLIE. My letter. *(Pause.)* Well, that must've been an old letter. I guess you didn't stop reading right away.

HELEN. No.

CHARLIE. Just stopped answering.

HELEN. Yeah.

CHARLIE. Yeah well the wooden boat idea, that was a Speck thing. Speck's idea, romantic and all but not exactly practical. So now she's some iron and some wood. *(Brandishes bottle.)* Anyway here's to the boat then, here's to Pinky, the Brave Little Schooner, the Little Schooner that — *(Helen kisses him. For a long time. Champagne goes everywhere. She doesn't leave his arms, just his mouth.)*

HELEN. *(In first breath.)* Well.

CHARLIE. Well that ... beats whittling.

HELEN. *(Laughs and takes bottle, still close to him.)* Nice work, Captain.

CHARLIE. You keep calling me that.

HELEN. I'm just proud of you is all.

CHARLIE. Proud. *(Withdraws.)* What're you so proud of?

HELEN. Don't be so suspicious.

CHARLIE. You think this had something to do with you? It had nothing to do with you.

HELEN. Hey, I know all right? Get off your high horse.

CHARLIE. You get off your high horse.

HELEN. What?

CHARLIE. Just quit being so PROUD of me. There's nothing for you to be proud of.

HELEN. Fine. Forget it.

CHARLIE. I'm not like I was before, Helen.

HELEN. Look. Just — high horses aside, you don't have anything left to prove. You built the boat.

CHARLIE. So?

HELEN. So you don't have to go sailing off to the bottom of the ocean or wherever the hell —

CHARLIE. I told you, SCOTLAND —

HELEN. Circum-goddamn navigation —

CHARLIE. Down this side then up the other side. Of the world. Not hard to work out, Helen.

HELEN. What if you need food? Or repairs? You can't pay for that. Or God forbid if you get another SPLINTER? Ya wuss? Ya pansy?

CHARLIE. You'd be surprised at the demand for a fellow can plank and caulk a ship's keel from scratch.

HELEN. Listen to you, caulk and plank a keel. What're you, the Ancient Friggin' Mariner?

CHARLIE. Or at how many girls can suck out a splinter.

HELEN. Okay. So you make it Scotland. What'll you do then? You'll be thirty-five when you get there.

CHARLIE. I'll decide when I get there.

HELEN. You'll be a bum.

CHARLIE. Well what am I now Helen?

HELEN. You're not a bum Charlie.

CHARLIE. Oh yeah?

HELEN. Not yet.

CHARLIE. Well that's not what you said before.

HELEN. You were living in your mother's basement before. *(Overlap.)* WE were living —

CHARLIE. And I'll be back in that basement tomorrow if I don't get on this boat.

HELEN. It's not the basement or the boat.

CHARLIE. It is for me.

HELEN. There are other things you can be.

CHARLIE. Like you? I could be like you?

HELEN. I wouldn't recommend it.

CHARLIE. I hear, you're a headhunter. I heard that's your job: headhunter.

HELEN. Is that what you heard.

CHARLIE. Well that sounds great. That sounds like a place where I'd love to work.

HELEN. Well where WOULD you work?

CHARLIE. Onward and upward, right?

HELEN. Where would you EVER work?

CHARLIE. Where I'm *gonna* work. Out there. On the water.

HELEN. Right, unless you're *in* the water, or *under*water.

CHARLIE. You know, everybody is happy for me except you.

HELEN. Is that right?

CHARLIE. Everybody has faith in me, except you.

HELEN. That's because nobody gives enough of a *shit* to set you *straight*, except me.

CHARLIE. And how're you setting me straight, coming back here —

HELEN. Because if you DIE in that thing, man, if you sink, if you get lost, if you get smashed like a bucket of eggs —

CHARLIE. I'm not gonna GET LOST.

HELEN. Like a bucket of eggs on the fuckin' rocks, then what the hell reason will I have to ever come here again?

CHARLIE. Same as now, so you can feel better than everybody else.

HELEN. Is that what you think?

CHARLIE. You're a snob here now. You're a tourist.

HELEN. Fine. Go off on your boat.

CHARLIE. I have to finish Speck first.

HELEN. Fuckin' Speck. *(Helen grabs Speck.)*

CHARLIE. Hey!

HELEN. Speck'll join you in the Bahamas. *(She grabs the whittling knife.)* You can go.

CHARLIE. Speck!

HELEN. But you won't. Because you're scared. *(On "scared," she jams the Swiss Army knife into the wood.)*

CHARLIE. Speck! *(Helen removes the knife, Charlie watches in horror.)* That's where his eye was gonna be! *(Helen pulls out the Swiss Army corkscrew, winds it into Speck.)* Holy God woman, what's wrong with you? *(She lobs Speck back to him.)* He's fuckin' blind in both eyes!

HELEN. Hey Charlie. *(She dangles upside down off the dock.)* Aren't you gone yet? Why aren't you gone yet?

CHARLIE. What're you doing?

HELEN. Sheilagh hangs off the roof so Alec'll listen, right? So can I make my point now?

CHARLIE. What point? You're being nuts! *(Helen gets him in a scissor hold with her legs and hauls him down.)*

HELEN. WHOORAGH!

CHARLIE. Holy shit! *(She jumps up, and is now dangling him off the dock.)* Holy fuck!

HELEN.   Now you listen to me, Charlie Blake. And excuse my Irish bullshit, but I'm a McNeil and the McNeils are *hardy Irish stock,* you smug Scot bastard. Now maybe I am a headhunter, but that's a talent I've got. And I like it. I'm proud of it. And you built this boat, Charlie. You got a gift. Now I saw how excited everybody got about the boat and the trip —

CHARLIE.   They're just glad to get rid of me is all —

HELEN.   *(Shakes him angrily.)* Knock it off! Knock it off or I swear to Jesus you're going into the drink.

CHARLIE.   Sorry. Sorry. Holy fuck.

HELEN.   I saw the whole town get behind the boat and the trip and you, too, Charlie. Charlie? *(Charlie snuffles.)* Are you crying?

CHARLIE.   No. The blood's all rushing to my head.

HELEN.   Oh.

CHARLIE.   So quit screwing around here and help me up. *(She does.)*

HELEN.   You don't have to do this Charlie.

CHARLIE.   Hey listen Helen I want to do this.

HELEN.   Do you? Because you don't seem that way to me. You seem scared.

CHARLIE.   I might be scared. So what?

HELEN.   Charlie I came back to tell you not to waste three more years.

CHARLIE.   What'll I do then, Helen? Hang around here? With Alec?

HELEN.   If you spend three years in that boat you're gonna *end up* like Alec.

CHARLIE.   I *am* like Alec. All right, Helen. I'm *just* like Alec. Alec is a bum, right? He's a waste. And this boat is my chance to not be that way. Anymore. And not end up like you. Ever.

HELEN.   So why don't you go then?

CHARLIE.   Well why should I stay? For you?

HELEN.   Well ... why not? *(Pause.)*

CHARLIE.   Hey, listen Helen, forget it. When I met you I was living in my mother's basement. And when you took off I was still in that basement. You didn't do a thing to me.

HELEN.   Thanks.

CHARLIE.   So you're off the hook.

HELEN.   Thanks. Thanks a bunch.

CHARLIE.   You believe me?

HELEN.   Sure. *(Chucks her bottle into the water behind them, looks to the party.)* You hear those voices? I know every voice up there tonight. Sheilagh. Alec. Your mother. I used to have a voice like that. I used to talk like that. It comes out of me, when I'm drunk. And one night, I got so drunk, I forgot where I was. I thought I was back on your street. I was all hammered, what did I know? I thought I could see your mother's house at the end of the road. And I even yelled out, "Hey Charlie!" Stupid, right? But I heard it. That voice. And when I left here I couldn't wait to get that way of talking out of me. But all drunk to hell that night, I thought I sounded pretty good. And a taxi went by and I thought, "Ah hell, there's no taxis in Mahone Bay." And I took the taxi back to my apartment, and my apartment was empty. And now I'm back. And I still feel gone. I'm sick of feeling like that. And I don't want it to happen to you. It happens when you leave.

CHARLIE. You gotta build a boat.

HELEN. Shut up.

CHARLIE. You're sick of it right? You said you're sick. Sick of food yet?

HELEN. No.

CHARLIE. You got a while yet then. You'll get sicker yet then.

HELEN. Shut up.

CHARLIE. Sick of food. I mean sick of eating, sick of all of it? That's the way I was in that basement. Down in the dark, all the time. But Helen, about a year after you left, something happened and it was, it was kind of a miracle. See my Uncle Speck came back to life. You remember the Whitecap Ranger?

HELEN. No.

CHARLIE. The Whitecap Ranger was an fishing trawler, went down off the coast of Newfoundland in 1978. Old Speck was a rigger on the Whitecap Ranger. And when that ship went down, when Speck went down, it was the worst day I could remember. Until you left I guess.

HELEN. But Speck came back.

CHARLIE. He came back Christmas morning. Dead for twenty-some years and we find him sitting under the Christmas tree. My mother knew him straight away. "Speck," she says, "you went down and died, where've you been all these years?" Speck just rolls out from under the tree and tells her, "Flossie, it's a long swim." Now I thought here's a man who swam back from the dead. Maybe he can help me climb out of the basement. So I said to him, I said, "Speck, what's the secret?" And he said, "Build me a boat, boy, and I'll tell you."

HELEN. So this is Speck's boat.

CHARLIE. Well it would've been but Speck died, for real, about two weeks later.

HELEN. What?

CHARLIE. Yeah, anchor through the belly.

HELEN. An anchor.

CHARLIE. Yeah. So. Anyway. Come springtime I started Speck's boat. Five o'clock every morning I was in my mother's driveway, drilling and soldering. I woke up everybody within earshot. Mahone Bay got up at dawn every day. I had a reason, not just to get up. I had a reason to get up early. It's still Speck's secret. A reason to get up early. His secret was the boat. See Helen, I really was different before I built this boat. I was old before. When you knew me, I was an old man. I'm young now. I'm finally a young man. *(Helen looks at him then looks back up the hill.)* Do you believe me? ... It would be good if you believed me. Helen? *(Helen pulls her to him and kisses him. It's quite a kiss. Charlie doesn't know what to say.)* Uh ... was that a yes kiss or a no kiss?

HELEN. *(Lets him go.)* Goodbye kiss.

CHARLIE. Oh. Well ... that's not quite fair, I mean, if I'd've known that was my *goodbye* kiss, I'd've put a little more into it, you know?

HELEN. That's all you get.

CHARLIE. Damn.

HELEN. It's close to dawn.

CHARLIE. It's close.

HELEN. Sorry about wrecking your whittling.

CHARLIE. Yeah. *(Considers, then exits and speaks from offstage.)* Well, you know, Alec gave me this for going away. *(Emerges with a jolly-looking garden gnome statue.)* Maybe it'll have to do. It actually looks a lot like Speck. *(Affixes gnome to the bow of the boat.)* There. Speck had a pretty good sense of humor. And I got to get going.

HELEN. You leaving now?

CHARLIE. Yeah. Goodbyes are ... well it's better just to leave quiet I think. *(Pause, eyes Helen.)* You didn't ... want to come along. Did you?

HELEN. Nah. I'm a landlubber. But you belong on your boat.

CHARLIE. You really think that?

HELEN. I know it.

CHARLIE. Thanks. *(Pause. Charlie looks to his boat.)* Scotland's waiting.

HELEN. Scotland waits. *(Gathers up her blanket around her.)* Well. I guess I'll watch you from up the hill.

CHARLIE. So long Helen.

HELEN. Bonne voyagee. Captain Blake. *(Helen exits. Charlie watches her go, his hand held up in a goodbye wave. He gets the anchor up. He moves over to the mast to hoist the sail. He pulls the rope down till the sail is all the way up. The sun shines on it.)*

End of Play

PROPERTY LIST

Champagne bottles
Block of wood, Swiss Army knife (CHARLIE)
Garden gnome (CHARLIE)
Blanket (HELEN)
Sail, rope, anchor (CHARLIE)

SOUND EFFECTS

Water lapping
Distant voices, party

D.C.
by Daria Polatin

CHARACTERS

MANDY, early teens; smart, really smart

WILBUR, also early teens; in all of Mandy's classes

MISS PASSIVO, their teacher, early thirties

PLACE

A classroom late after school.
Cedar Slope High School, U.S.A.

TIME

The present.

D.C.

Lights fade up on a classroom after school. Late after school. It is Cedar Slope High. There are many open dictionaries and two full backpacks strewn about the room. There is a map of the world on the wall and an American flag. We see two young teenagers, Mandy and Wilbur. Wilbur wears oversized, out-of-date clothing. Mandy is dressed slightly cooler than he. Just slightly.

MANDY. Hit me.

WILBUR. Okay — Algonquin.

MANDY. Algonquin. A.L.G.O.N.Q.U.I.N. Algonquin. Easy. *(They are moving and stretching as if preparing for a sports game.)*

WILBUR. Okay — zoologist.

MANDY. Zoologist. Z.O.O.L.O.G.I.S.T. Zoologist. Kid's stuff. Challenge me, Wilbur, challenge me.

WILBUR. Okay, I'm trying Mandy. Umm, stenophagous.

MANDY. Stenophagous. S.T.E.N.O.P.H.A.G.O.U.S. Stenophagous. Your turn.

WILBUR. Okay. I'm ready.

MANDY. I'll start out easy. Shenanigan.

WILBUR. Shenanigan ... shenanigan ...

MANDY. What are you doing?

WILBUR. Sometimes I just have to say the word to myself a few times to, you know, see it.

MANDY. The judges will see that as a weakness. Say it inside your head.

WILBUR. Okay. *(He says it inside his head.)* Shenanigan. S.H.E.N.A.N.I.G.A.N. Shenanigan.

MANDY. Good. Oligarchy.

WILBUR. Okay, oligarchy. O.L.I.G.A.R.C.H.Y. Oligarchy.

MANDY. Tanganyika.

WILBUR. What the hell is that?

MANDY. A town in Africa. Go.

WILBUR. They're not gonna ask that.

MANDY. Spell it!

WILBUR. Tanganyika. T.A.N. *(Pause.)* G.A.N. *(Pause.)* Y.I.C? K? A. Tanganyika?

MANDY. I can't believe you.

WILBUR. I'm sorry. That was a hard one.

MANDY. And you don't think there will be hard ones in Washington? How do you expect to change the world, Wilbur, unless we can win this spelling bee and get to the president and tell him how we feel? How are we going to tell him that the way this world is going now is in no place to be passed down to our children?

WILBUR. But we don't have any child —

MANDY. That's not the point. The point is, we've got to go to D.C., nip this thing in the bud, and when we're shaking the president's hand, pull him aside and say, "Listen, Mr. President: We've got to talk. Things have got to change around this country. To start out, the educational system is crap, the taxes are totally unfair, and there's hardly any ozone left. And don't even get me started on foreign policy. Things have got to change around this world, and we've got some ideas."

WILBUR. We do?

MANDY. Of course we do. That paper you wrote in philosophy last year: "Shifting The Ebb and Flow of Our Socioeconomic Tides"? There were some really good ideas in there.

WILBUR. Thanks. And you did do a kick-ass job on your "Equality For The Not-So-Athletically Gifted" impromptu presentation in gym.

MANDY. Well, the teams weren't fair.

WILBUR. I know.

MANDY. So this is a crucial time. A crucial moment in our lives.

WILBUR. Okay, yeah. It is crucial. C.R.U.C.I.A.L. Crucial. *(He laughs. She laughs, too.)*

MANDY. Crucial. Which reminds me. I have to ask Miss Passivo how close we are actually staying to the White House.

WILBUR. Why?

MANDY. No reason. Let's get back to business. Pitfalls —

WILBUR. I before E, except after C.

MANDY. Or when sounding like A, as in neighbor and weigh.

WILBUR. And never fall for the old *rasp*berry trick. That is the oldest one in the book.

MANDY. True, true. Very true. Always stay —

MANDY and WILBUR. Calm, cool and collected. *(They high five.)*

WILBUR. And of course, always say the word before and after spelling it.

MANDY. Right. It's as important as "what is" on *Jeopardy*. Right, Mr. Trebec?

WILBUR. Why yes it is, Amanda.

MANDY. Don't call me Amanda.

WILBUR. I was just kidding. You called me Alex Trebec and he's like the biggest dork ever, okay?

MANDY. Did you ever notice that you say "okay," like, all the time?

WILBUR. Umm, okay. I don't think that is very nice of you to be pointing out my faults at a time like this, okay?

MANDY. Well, it just makes you sound, like, not as smart as you really are.

WILBUR. Do you really think I'm smart, Mandy?

MANDY. Like, yeah.

WILBUR. Really?

MANDY. Wilbur, remember how I got a perfect score on the P.S.A.T.s?

WILBUR. Of course. We both aced it.

MANDY. Well, I didn't. I just said that 'cause I wanted you to think that I was smarter than you.

WILBUR. Okay, wow. I never thought you thought I was smart! And ... you do! *(Wilbur hugs her. An awkward moment.)*

MANDY. Whoa.

WILBUR. Oh, okay. I mean sorry, not okay. Umm ... something.

MANDY. You scored, like, the highest of anyone I know.

WILBUR. Thanks.

MANDY. Even higher than Edgar.

WILBUR. Edgar?

MANDY. Yeah, and he's president of the student council.

WILBUR. I know ... I wrote his campaign speech.

MANDY. We'd better get back to work.

WILBUR. Yeah. You're right, Mandy. You always are.

MANDY. I know. We've got a contest to win.

WILBUR. And a world to change.

MANDY. We do.

WILBUR. I can't wait.

MANDY. Do you have any binoculars?

WILBUR. What?

MANDY. Never mind. Hit me.

WILBUR. All right … Let's see. How about … xystus.

MANDY. Xystus. Xys-tus.

WILBUR. I'll give you a hint. It's not S.I.S.T.A.S.

MANDY. Not funny.

WILBUR. Sorry. Okay, xystus.

MANDY. Xystus. *(A moment.)*

WILBUR. I thought you wanted to be ch —

MANDY. Xystus. X. *(Pause.)* Y. *(Pause.)* S.T.U.S. Xystus.

WILBUR. Well done. Okay … how about … oh, say, Rhynchocephalian.

MANDY. Okay … rhynchocephalian. *(She takes a deep breath. Wilbur hums the* Jeopardy *tune.)*

MANDY. Rhynchocephalian. R.H.Y.N., C., H.?,O., C.?, E.?, *(Pause.)* P.H.A.L.I.A.N. Rhynchocephalian. *(A moment. Wilbur shakes his head.)*

WILBUR. It sounded like you said M instead of N at the end.

MANDY. I so said N.

WILBUR. I know, but it sounded like M.

MANDY. I said N. N! You are so wrong.

WILBUR. All I'm saying is that I heard M and if we were competing right now, you wouldn't have made it past the regionals.

MANDY. That is such B.S. Plus, Edgar has a pen pal from agriculture camp who said that the regionals are so cinchy. The judges aren't even that strict. Why else do you think Miss Passivo is so confident in our success that she is sending us directly to the finals in Washington? Because she knows how smart we are. I'm smart, Wilbur, I know the difference between M and N!

WILBUR. Well, if you're so smart why don't you just do "the bee" by yourself. Better yet, do it with Edgar. After all, he's the president of the stupid student council. You probably told him about this whole thing anyway after we swore to secrecy.

MANDY. I did not tell him anything. And how dare you. The student council is not stupid! And Edgar is … Edgar is —

WILBUR. Edgar is what? *(Miss Passivo, a young teacher, bursts into the room. She's drunk.)*

MISS PASSIVO. Stop yelling! *(Mandy and Wilbur freeze.)* Are you two the new T.A.'s? Let me tell you: faculty meetings are the most idiotic thing in — Wait a minute — What the hell are you kids still doing here?

MANDY. Nothing, Miss Passivo.

MISS PASSIVO. Shouldn't you be at home with your parents or something? *(She goes to her desk to get something from the drawer.)*

WILBUR. Well, actually my parents work late, so I wouldn't really be home, you know, with them?

MISS PASSIVO. What?

MANDY. We were just doing some research.

WILBUR. Yeah, for the final.

MISS PASSIVO. The final? There is no — What are all these dictionaries doing out?

MANDY. We had to look something up for —

MISS PASSIVO. You were preparing for that National Spelling Bee again, weren't you?

WILBUR. No, okay?

MISS PASSIVO. Because I told you not to.

WILBUR. Of course not, Miss Passivo.

MISS PASSIVO. Good. I'm glad someone still listens to me.

MANDY. Yes. Yes we are. We didn't tell anyone about it, like you said, but we're preparing for the spelling bee because we are going to win it, hands down.

MISS PASSIVO. You're going to win it hands down?

MANDY. *(Hesitates.)* Yeah.

WILBUR. Yeah. We're going to win it — me and Mandy.

MISS PASSIVO. Me and Mandy? I expected more from you, Mr. Ryder.

WILBUR. It's Schneider.

MISS PASSIVO. How do you know you're going to win it? How do you know you're going to win it hands down? How do you know?

MANDY. Because ... I'm a good speller.

WILBUR. And, like, the smartest one in the school.

MISS PASSIVO. And you don't think there may be smarter people out there, Miranda?

MANDY. Amanda.

MISS PASSIVO. How'd you get in here anyway? I thought I locked the door.

WILBUR. *(Mumbles.)* Window.

MISS PASSIVO. What?

MANDY. Second window from the left. You always leave it unlocked. He climbed in then opened the door from the inside.

MISS PASSIVO. You kids think you know everything. Well, let me tell you: You don't. There ain't no spelling bee. There ain't no trip to Washington or wherever I told you it was.

MANDY and WILBUR. What?

MISS PASSIVO. There is no spelling bee. I just told you that so you would get off my back to start that political science club thing you wanted to do. Damn overachievers.

WILBUR. There's no Spelling Bee?

MISS PASSIVO. No. Plus, aren't you a little old to be doing spelling bees? If you're so goddamned smart how come you didn't do a little more research and figure out that the cut-off age is fourteen? Huh?

MANDY. So we're not going to meet the president?

WILBUR. Okay, why did you tell us that there was a spelling bee when there wasn't one?

MANDY. Yeah. This is an outrage. You provided false information. You're not supposed to do that. I'm telling Principal Hardly and he'll bring it to the board of education and —

MISS PASSIVO. And what, Amanda?

MANDY. And … and …

MISS PASSIVO. And … they'll fire me? Do you know how hard it is to find teachers these days, honey? He'll never believe you anyway. Weren't you the ones that staged a fake protest in the quad so you could raid the cafeteria?

WILBUR. *(The following is pronounced as a word, not spelled.)* It was for U.N.I.C.E.F!

MANDY. For starving children.

MISS PASSIVO. Which reminds me; they're waiting for me at Knickerbockers. I can't be too late, or I'll miss "Dante's Inferno Shots." See ya kids. Do me a favor and get out of here soon so the janitor can give this place a good clean, okay? Bye. *(She leaves.)*

MANDY. I thought he might leave the First Lady …

WILBUR. What? Mandy, you're talking crazy. Come on, let's get back to work. Miss Passivo probably just told us that so we wouldn't rat it to the other kids.

MANDY. It's ruined, Wilbur. It's all ruined.

WILBUR. No it's not. I'm sure there still is some spelling bee somewhere, okay?

MANDY. Forget it. It's not gonna happen.

WILBUR. I guess you're right. But wait a minute, Mandy: Do you think you want to go anyway?

MANDY. Where?

WILBUR. D.C.

MANDY. You mean, just go there?

WILBUR. Yeah, we could just go there, you and I, and maybe try to change some of the things we talked about, you know? Try to get things done? Make things a little better?

MANDY. And leave Cedar Slope? I have that presentation on photosynthesis to give on Friday, and the chess team really needs me for the training on Sunday.

WILBUR. Oh. Okay. *(Pause.)* Are you sure?

MANDY. D.C. was just a dream, Wilbur. We're never gonna get to really go there.

WILBUR. But we could make sandwiches and get on a bus and —

MANDY. I don't think so.

WILBUR. Why not?

MANDY. Wilbur, how are we supposed to change the world? We don't even have credit cards.

WILBUR. Well, what do we need to have? I mean, we're smart, right? And we have really good ideas. *(Beat.)* Well, maybe I'll go, Mandy.

MANDY. Where?

WILBUR. Maybe I'll go to D.C. and get some things done around this country.

MANDY. What? You can't just go to D.C.

WILBUR. Why not? What have I got to lose? There's nothing for me here.

MANDY. But you haven't even finished high school.

WILBUR. You said yourself the educational system is crap.

MANDY. Yeah, but I didn't mean it like that.

WILBUR. Well, how did you mean it? *(No answer.)* I think it's time I took matters into my own hands.

MANDY. If you go, who's gonna write winning speeches for the debate team?

WILBUR. Anyone in A.P. English can do that.

MANDY. Who's gonna be in charge of the tambourines in gospel choir?

WILBUR. Lenny's got rhythm.

MANDY. Well, who's gonna be my partner for the Humanities project? And who's gonna walk home with me when I get out of the library late and it's dark out? And who's gonna hold a newspaper over my head in the rain?

WILBUR. You had that new haircut and I didn't want it to get all messed up.

MANDY. I know. *(A moment.)*

WILBUR. I thought you were working on humanities with Mr. Student Council.

MANDY. I'm not. I want you to be my partner.

WILBUR. Okay, I guess. But only under one condition.

MANDY. What?

WILBUR. That you let me talk to you in the hallways.

MANDY. Umm —

WILBUR. Where's Greyhound?

MANDY. Yes ... of course. Edgar's such a nerd anyway.

WILBUR. Really? I thought he was so cool.

MANDY. Nah. I was only hanging out with him because he said he'd make me his running mate next year.

WILBUR. Oh.

MANDY. Plus he has a lisp.

WILBUR. *(Laughs.)* I know.

MANDY. *(Laughs too.)* It's pretty funny.

WILBUR. Yeah ...

MANDY. So ... I'll see you tomorrow in trig?

WILBUR. I do have to give a tutoring session before school anyway ... I guess we're needed here, right?

MANDY. Right. We're needed here. You're needed here.

WILBUR. I guess that's good.

MANDY. Yeah, it probably is good.

WILBUR. Okay. Bye.

MANDY. Goodbye. *(Wilbur starts to leave.)*

WILBUR. Mandy?

MANDY. Yeah?

WILBUR. Thanks.

MANDY. Yeah.

WILBUR. Okay. *(He starts to leave again.)*

MANDY. Wilbur?

WILBUR. Yeah?

MANDY. We're gonna kick ass in humanities.

WILBUR. Yeah ... we will. *(Wilbur leaves. Mandy takes a moment and looks around the room. She slowly puts on her backpack, hooks her thumbs in the straps, and takes a big breath. She sighs, and leaves.)*

End of Play

PROPERTY LIST

Dictionaries
2 backpacks
Map of the world
American flag

WELCOME BACK, BUDDY COMBS
by Ben Rosenthal

CHARACTERS

BUDDY COMBS, a discharged marine, late twenties

BEVERLY COMBS, his wife

WYNNE FRANKLIN, their friend

SETTING

A small one-bedroom row house in the Northeast.

WELCOME BACK, BUDDY COMBS

Bud and Beverly's house. Living room. Night. The lights are off. There is a fold out bed. A key turns in the door and Bud enters in marine regalia with a small suitcase. He sets it down and turns the light on.

BUD. Hello? Beverly? Beverly? Honey? I'm home. It's Bud. *(The toilet flushes and Wynne enters from bathroom with a beer in his hand, wearing a British tweed hat.)* Wynne? *(Pause.)*
WYNNE. Hail fellow, well met.
BUD. Wynne, you're — is Beverly...?
WYNNE. Hail fellow, well met.
BUD. That's right ... Thirteen weeks of boot camp sewn up. Complete. What you doin' here, Wynne?
WYNNE. Hail fellow, well met.
BUD. Why you saying this, Wynne?
WYNNE. What brings you back here, Bud?
BUD. Discharge. Um. Honorable.
WYNNE. Thought you'd stick it out.
BUD. I did. Wynne, aren't you excited to see me?
WYNNE. I'm hanging from the proverbial rafter, Bud.
BUD. Well ...
WYNNE. Bev's out on some small detail of buying pantyhose.
BUD. Is she?
WYNNE. Last ones got nicked in a hurry. Lemme tell you, you bend that girl over a sawhorse, she'll howl if you know her right.
BUD. Are you ... am I ... *Wynne? (Beverly enters from outside, shuts door behind her, turns around and sees Bud.)*
BEVERLY. Bud. You're home.
BUD. Beverly, what's goin' on?
BEVERLY. I'm so unbelievably happy to see you.
BUD. Good to be home.
BEVERLY. You look so ... unscruffed.
BUD. Corps can do that.
BEVERLY. I just find it amazing you're home.

71

BUD. What have you been up to?

BEVERLY. Refurbishing. Wynne's helped. *(Bud takes a look.)*

BUD. Wynne's been awful occupied around here.

WYNNE. Someone has to show work in the face of desuetude.

BUD. What's that word mean?

WYNNE. Sort of chronic disuse.

BUD. Things been disused around here?

WYNNE. Some things been undernourished. Been getting butter-flies around the prospect you would come back here, Bud, trawl-ing in like a U.S. slave. You done good by conscripting your spirit to the forces of freedom.

BUD. I'm a little fuzzy on your attitude, Wynne.

WYNNE. I'm a little whirled up on your presence.

BUD. I live here.

WYNNE. Bev lives here.

BUD. With me.

WYNNE. We've just stumbled onto something grave. *(Pause.)*

BEVERLY. It only happened six or seven times before we knew it was love.

WYNNE. Oh, I knew at once.

BEVERLY. Did you?

WYNNE. Oh, right away. Bev calls me over to fix the drain back-up. So there I am in my little Civic, sitting in your driveway con-templating the disuse of my Franklin ...

BUD. Your ... Franklin. You ... still call your wick your Franklin?

WYNNE. My Franklin has not seen much oxygen since Mary left me. There I am. In the driveway. Night herons in the trees. A Chinese palm-rolling ball ringing in my ears ...

BEVERLY. Rain on his windshield ...

WYNNE. I'm sitting, thinking, "What would Bud think of my position?" Fix the drain.

BEVERLY. I wave him in.

WYNNE. I enter sopping and cold.

BEVERLY. And isn't water a sex metaphor?

WYNNE. ... and just at that moment, like telepathy, Bev kicks into play. It was her, Bud.

BEVERLY. *(Slaps Wynne with a flailing wrist.)* Oh stop, Wynnie, stop playing blame game right now.

WYNNE. We have our moments in the sheets. It feels a might dirty ...

BEVERLY. ... because he gets uncomfortable with me on top ... I say, "You don't want to see my face, you can turn me around … "

WYNNE. … but, as we develop a confidence the only harbingers in our life seem like dead herons. They keep cropping up, dropping down on the lawn outside as we make love. We name each heron after you, Bud. Bud One and Bud Two and Bud Three. So on. After awhile there are so many damned Buds peppering the lawn we decide it's a colony. The Dead Heron Colony. Crows … are unwelcome. *(Bud lunges at Wynne and Beverly. He is about to take a swing at Beverly when Wynne grabs his arm and holds him back.)* You don't want that, Bud. Consider the love.

BUD. The love?

WYNNE. The blessed and forthright pitch of our love.

BUD. Isn't love. You guys are fucking around!

WYNNE. Bud, is it love? I'll let you go if you say it's love.

BEVERLY. Bud, just say it's love.

BUD. Jesus Christ!

BEVERLY. Say it, Bud, I don't like watching him hurt you.

BUD. You fucking sonofabitch, how can you…?

WYNNE. You'll just have to stop writhing.

BEVERLY. Bud, look at me.

BUD. Yeah?

BEVERLY. Look at me.

BUD. I'm looking. *(Beverly pulls out a ball of confetti and an accordion-like "Welcome Home" sign.)*

BEVERLY. Welcome home, Buddy Combs! You're on *Candid Camera!* *(Wynne begins laughing hysterically, lets go of Bud. Pause. Bud takes things in. Beverly throws her arms around him.)*

BUD. Are you…? Serious? This is … a joke? It's a joke?

WYNNE. Hey, get your hands off my woman. *(He smacks Bud on the back.)* Army life has made you one gullible mutt.

BUD. You guys, I can't believe you.

WYNNE. We really made you stung.

BUD. Oh yeah.

WYNNE. You were shittin'.

BUD. Oh you guys.

BEVERLY. Welcome home, Bud, really.

BUD. I can't believe you! I need a drink. Where's the Makers Mark? Where is the Jim fucking Beam?

WYNNE. I dunno, guy, this is your place.

BUD. Oh really? Thank you, thank you, Wynne. Let's see you fix me five fingers of bourbon, you plumb nut … You fucken' assholes …

BEVERLY. Now come on.

BUD. I think I'm fit to be jiggered.

WYNNE. It's a hard sell, we sold it ...

BUD. Oh yes, you did.

WYNNE. How 'bout that little speech?

BUD. Oh! Oh my God, that — where did you come up with that, Wynne? You goddamned Nazis! *(Wynne and Beverly laugh boisterously.)* Prank Nazis. *(Beverly wraps her arms around Bud.)*

BEVERLY. Oh, Buddy, Buddy, my space-walking Apollo moon man.

BUD. The Eagle has landed. *(Wynne goes to bar, starts making drink.)*

WYNNE. Missed you, Bud. Your total immersion in the corps has left me without a bowling partner.

BUD. Handsome fucken' Nazi bastard. Handsome Wynne Franklin.

WYNNE. It's real good having you home, Bud.

BEVERLY. You know, Buddy, we've tried to keep busy bowling so when you came back ...

WYNNE. ... that's right, that is right ...

BEVERLY. Wynne's been rolling seven tens ...

BUD. Have you?

BEVERLY. Six or seven brews in him, he's capable of anything! You should see it ...

WYNNE. Feel something like a bowling lane Bobby Fischer these days, you should see the rolls ...

BEVERLY. Three of us should really go one night. Oh Buddy, Buddy, Buddy, my puckered grunt cutie wootie, making his army corners and bouncing quarters off of cots. Bud Combs. I'm so happy you're home. Those army officials don't know a good man when they see him. *(As Beverly says this she is tugging at Wynne's arm. Pause.)*

BUD. Builds character.

WYNNE. I envy you, Bud, my character is in want of a rehab clinic.

BUD. *(Jabs Wynne.)* You flunky punk.

WYNNE. *(Clicks heels, salutes.)* Sir, yes sir.

BUD. Well, let's have that Beam, Wynne. *(Wynne gives Bud drink. He sips, walks over to Beverly, grabs her.)* And *you.* Speaking of bouncing quarters. You wonder what to do with yourself while I was away?

BEVERLY. Oh, I found ways.

BUD. Oh yeah? Ways. What's that?

WYNNE. *(Laughing.)* Hey, Bud, don't look at *me.*

BUD. *(Laughing.)* ... Hey, pal, I'm trying not to!

BEVERLY. Bud, there are more things you can do with a cucumber than make a pickle.

BUD. Oh yeah?

WYNNE. Bud, you ask nice, she might stick it up your coolie. *(He laughs to himself. Pause.)*

BUD. *(Gives Wynne a look of death.)* You know, Wynne, you uh, aren't all that funny tonight.

WYNNE. I'm sorry.

BUD. You know that?

WYNNE. Yeah, I'm, you're right; that was one dot over the line. You know, I'm pretty well potted here, Bud. *(Pause. Bud smiles and slings his thumb and forefinger out at Wynne.)*

BUD. Gotcha!

WYNNE. Oh, man ... You got me when I'm soft. Been going through fifth flasks like it was tap water all night.

BEVERLY. *(To Bud, laughing hysterically.)* He has. He's so funny when he's drunk. *(Laughter dies down. Bud, about to take a pleasant sip, stops the ascent of his glass somewhere beneath his chin; his expression freezes.)*

BUD. So you been here all night?

WYNNE. Wh...? Yeah, waiting on *you.*

BUD. What you been doin'?

BEVERLY. ... Bud ...

BUD. Just, seems a little bizarre you sharing this railroad space with Bev all night ... with all you guys pulled ...

WYNNE. Bud, it was a *joke* ...

BEVERLY. ... it was a joke, Bud ...

WYNNE. Come on, Bud, what they do to you there? They simonize your brain? Embalm your sense of humor? We were having some fun.

BUD. Just went a little far is all.

WYNNE. Bud, we thought you knew us well enough ...

BEVERLY. I need a goddamn cigarette if you're keeping *this* up.

BUD. Yeah, yeah. I'm sorry.

WYNNE. Besides, Bev, you really oughta watch your streak.

BUD. What streak is this?

WYNNE. Oh, she didn't tell you? *(Short pause.)*

BUD. No, no, she didn't tell me. Haven't been kept apprised, but you can tell me, Wynne.

WYNNE. Well, I think Beverly ought to be the one.

BUD. You're probably right. *(Pause.)*

BEVERLY. *(Breaking a terrible silence.)* I quit. There it is. I quit.

BUD. Oh. Congratulations.

BEVERLY. Well, Wynne helped.

BUD. Did he?

BEVERLY. He had this little speech when I was teetering on resuming, you know. It was ... *(Wynne steps forward.)*

WYNNE. Shall I?

BEVERLY. Oh please, you're much better verbally ...

WYNNE. *No.*

BEVERLY. *Yes.*

WYNNE. Well, okay, princess. So, Bev would get so swept up by the illness of nicotine, after a day or two of not smoking.

BEVERLY. You've never seen me so emotionally naked ...

WYNNE. She'd say, "Wynne. Help me stop."

BEVERLY. *(Laughs.)* He'd say, "Bev, you know when you're taking smoke from those little white narcotizing tubes, think of it this way: They're not a million minuscule grounds of tar and other manmade field crop articles from the Carolinas; they're earmites."

WYNNE. "You're inhaling earmites."

BEVERLY. "And not *just* earmites. Communist consortium earmites."

WYNNE. "Labor Party rug dwellers."

BEVERLY. "With Joseph Stalin mustaches."

WYNNE. "And Karl Marx goatees. *(Steps forward.)* And while Bud is out learning to defend the world against the oncoming throngs of Communism you're harboring the future world brigands of the proletariat ... "

BEVERLY. "The million meek who shall inherit every acre Bud pledges to defend on account of Uncle Sam ... "

WYNNE. "And Audie Murphy ... "

BEVERLY. "And the wondrous undefiled bunting of the red, white and blue!"

WYNNE. I don't think she ever thought about hand-tamping a pack of Luckies after that little number, Bud! *(They laugh.)*

BEVERLY. It's true ...

BUD. *(Trying to laugh.)* That's, that's great.

WYNNE. Isn't it?

BEVERLY. *(To Wynne.)* Anyway, gimme a cigarette. *(She and Wynne break into knee-slapping laughter. This goes on for some time.)*

BUD. What's ... what's going on here?

BEVERLY. *(Still laughing.)* Oh ... *(She turns to Bud.)* What do you mean?

BUD. Well, I mean, you guys are like thick as thieves ...

BEVERLY. Are we? I didn't notice.

WYNNE. What are you sayin', Bud?

BUD. Well, you come with this joke, but, it doesn't much seem like a joke from my angle here ... is what I'm saying. I mean I wonder if the protocol is I should leave right now so you can fuck on my rug ...

BEVERLY. Jesus, Bud.

BUD. Well, I dunno.

WYNNE. Bud, be careful.

BUD. Be *careful? Me?*

WYNNE. It. Was. A. Joke.

BUD. I'm just not so damned sure, Wynnie, not so convinced.

WYNNE. And how is that?

BUD. You seemed awful sure of yourself pulling it off. You telling it. It was like more than rehearsed. You aren't all that gifted an actor, Wynne. You two seem awful convinced you fell in some kind of *love* here.

BEVERLY. Bud, we didn't sleep together.

BUD. I ... maybe you didn't but ...

BEVERLY. What, then?

BUD. I dunno man. This is like, if you didn't sleep together it damn well seems you want to.

WYNNE. Oh come on, Bud.

BUD. No, you come on. You went over the grizzly details, you must have known what you were saying.

WYNNE. Yeah?

BUD. And if you knew what you were saying that means you two thought about it, to know what you were saying. Long and hard. And if you ... Did you go over this story *together?*

BEVERLY. Yes.

BUD. God fucking damnit!

BEVERLY. ... so *what?*

BUD. "So what" is you guys were rolling over fucking each other behind my back. In all sorts of gymnastic ways of *fucking behind my back.* You think that's a source of comfort?! And the way you two are consorting here in front of me, it's like you guys are fucking right here.

WYNNE. Bud, you're losing focus.

BUD. *Focus?*

WYNNE. We're just friends.

BUD. Well, I'd sure like you guys to throw this friendship back a notch. Jesus fucking Christ.

WYNNE. I'm sorry.

BUD. Yeah, you *should* be sorry.

WYNNE. Well, I am.

BEVERLY. We both are.

WYNNE. Really are ...

BEVERLY. ... really are sorry, Bud.

WYNNE. Bud, you know me. I'm Wynne Franklin of Red Oak Lane in Wiltontown. Whom you sold lemonade with? Who does not forsake his friends. We really were just having a gas.

BEVERLY. Just a gas ...

WYNNE. You're always tailgating my sentences ...

BEVERLY. ... sentences. *(The two laugh together.)*

BUD. It isn't right.

WYNNE. Isn't right? What's the precedent here? I seem to recall a time in high school you convinced me you saw my dad French-kissing a man back of the Caldors' dumpster. Had me going. Had everybody going. I remember confronting my father, in sheer desperation, asking him if he was a queer right in front of his business partners ...

BUD. I know that ...

WYNNE. And countless occasions ... .

BUD. ... fine, Wynne ...

WYNNE. Of friendly, inconsequential pranks. Fraternal pranks. Don't become like some coot, here, Bud.

BUD. All right.

WYNNE. 'Cause I won't have it.

BEVERLY. He's fine, Wynne. Bud, we were just razzing you. Nobody's out to hurt you. You're fine.

WYNNE. So, how about a group hug. Huhm? *(Pause.)*

BUD. Yeah. All right. Yeah. *(The three draw in.)*

WYNNE. So which one of us fucks Beverly first? *(They draw apart. Bud stares crossly. Beverly laughs in an overcompensating way.)*

BEVERLY. That's *enough*, Wynne.

WYNNE. I know, I know. *(Turns from Beverly.)* You know, you got a real good woman here, Bud.

BUD. You still kidding, Wynne?

WYNNE. I could be. How would *you* know? Bud, the premature

old coot.

BUD. Ha ha! Now get out of here, I wanna fuck my wife as I'm properly qualified, you lily-livered Judas. I'll be the one making her into an animal tonight. I'll make her into the whore she rightly is!

BEVERLY. *Hey.*

BUD. What?

BEVERLY. Would both you guys shut up. I'm not some chattel here. Jesus H. *Christ.*

WYNNE. Yeah, Bud, what's on your mind?

BUD. Me?

WYNNE. That was a little unnecessary.

BUD. You are joking, right? *(Pause.)*

WYNNE. Yeah. Guess. I don't know. Yes fine. I will say I am joking.

BUD. I just tread on some delicate feeling you have for Bev?

WYNNE. Called her a *whore,* Bud.

BEVERLY. Wynne, I'll ... be all right.

BUD. You got some problem, Wynne? *(Wynne sits down, takes hat off.)* You wanna fuck my wife? 'Cause I got a feeling here you both want it. You thought this would be funny? You didn't think I'd get mad?

WYNNE. Didn't *think,* Bud. I mean at first maybe you'd be a little pissed but ...

BUD. I'd get over it. See, I think that the only way you could go ahead with this little whim is if the price a pissing me off wasn't as much as the relief in explaining me how you feel ...

BEVERLY. No, Bud, listen ... *(Pause. Turns to Wynne.)*

BUD. Got something for my wife?

WYNNE. I Do Not Wish To Be Cornered For A Joke! *(Long pause. Defiantly.)* Yeah, all right, maybe. Maybe I do. It was a joke. It was a pleasant Alan Funt style joke. But, I guess since you're so disposed to calling me on it, Jesus. I don't know. I'm going to quit before I'll jam my foot right down my throat ...

BUD. What about you, Beverly?

BEVERLY. Bud, don't make me say things I'll regret.

BUD. I can't believe this!

BEVERLY. Bud ...

BUD. What?

BEVERLY. You were away.

BUD. So you did ... So it *wasn't* a joke ... So you did. You ... two ...

BEVERLY. We Just Joked About It. We Joked About It! All month we had it in the offing. But it was all a joke.

WYNNE. *(Softly.)* Maybe he's right. *(Pause.)*

BEVERLY. What?

WYNNE. Beverly, maybe you and me have been kidding ourselves here. Look into my eyes.

BEVERLY. Don't do that to me, Wynne, right now.

WYNNE. ... look into my eyes and tell me all the while Bud is away you're never dreaming it. All our coded exchanges lead by hindsight to Bud's conclusion.

BEVERLY. Wynne, you really should go home ...

BUD. No, no, Bev, I'd like to know. If my wife is feeling unto-ward. If she's having these feelings. I'd like to know. You might as well say it. I'm your *husband,* after all.

BEVERLY. I'm not going to say something stupid, Bud, because you want me to.

BUD. Yes then.

BEVERLY. *You* said it.

BUD. All right, Wynne, I'd like you to leave now ...

WYNNE. ... Bud ...

BUD. You get out of this house! *(Bud picks up any object he can find and hits the wall with it. Wynne begins slipping out towards the door, turns.)*

WYNNE. Fine.

BEVERLY. You really should sleep on this, Wynne.

WYNNE. *I won't sleep on this.* You wish me to say I have devel-oped feelings ... for your wife? Because of the prank we played ... I'm not incapable of ... Bud ... you're being ... decidedly unfair ... here ... you see me here ... your oldest friend ...

BEVERLY. Wynne ...

BUD. Beverly ...

WYNNE. All of this is making me very close to you, Beverly. Extremely at ease with the idea that maybe something, I dunno, Bud, Bev, would have happened but we didn't materialize it ...

BEVERLY. Stop. It means nothing. Wynne, you've no idea what you're saying. You're becoming reckless.

WYNNE. Now look at this woman. You can understand some nominal attraction.

BEVERLY. ... Wynne, you're making a spectacle of yourself. You enjoy being a person of dignity and we all see it. Now be somewhat proper and leave me and Bud here. We'll call you. Right, Bud?

BUD. Yeah. We'll call you, Wynne, just go to fucking sleep. *(He*

walks over to Bud, stands in his face.)
WYNNE. Try and embarrass me, Bud? Didn't cut it, did you? While there in your stint … You washed out … You didn't make it. You tramp on in here … Fine woman left to the wolves. I never wanted to hurt you. Maybe it's just … my native charm. *(Wynne laughs, dunks some more whiskey. Hands Bud the glass of whiskey. He waves a knowing finger at her, then salutes Bud, who is suddenly brought to charging at the door but Wynne exits. Bud slams it shut. He turns to Beverly. Long Pause.)*
BEVERLY. I'm sorry.
BUD. Oh you're sorry. I should pound you through the fucking wall!
BEVERLY. Bud …
BUD. Huh?
BEVERLY. Just calm.
BUD. You're leaving me? You are some real sick bitch, Bev, having this cooked for my arrival. So you tell me.
BEVERLY. You go away, things came to light. It was still a joke.
BUD. You *slept* with him.
BEVERLY. No, I didn't.
BUD. Yes, you did. What else would you call it?!
BEVERLY. I don't know. Impure thoughts.
BUD. Impure marriage, Bev, the whole thing's sullied …
BEVERLY. Don't say that. Bud, listen, you've, this, you've completely blown this open —
BUD. *I've* blown this…?
BEVERLY. *Yes.*
BUD. Do you love him?
BEVERLY. What?
BUD. 'Cause if you do I have to wonder what I'm looking at.
BEVERLY. Bud, it isn't that.
BUD. … and I have to stand here like a fucking monkey; you, you can't even look in my eyes. Now you answer me now, above this piddlin' shit, nothing left to the horse races! You explain this if something is stirring in you. You think of Wynne? It's the easiest thing to say and it'll all be over. You want him so much? You all but said it. Say it. Come on, Bev, you tell me if you think of him…!
BEVERLY. Yes. Yes, Bud, like your suspicions confirmed? I'll do it. You asked for it: I confess. Your friend Wynne has got a wonderful eye-popping shit-eating grin. Men mostly find it despicable but I'd dive inside it and swim. His shoulders beat yours. His eyes tell me more. They change like mood rings and everyday there is a new secret. And he has grace, Bud, some real masculine grace. He

moves the gearshift like a ballet dancer and you flop around all day like a belly-up fish. He makes me feel full to think about. All right? His eyes and nose and mouth and I want to fuck him, Bud. Really fuck him without a bed sheet. Ripe enough to break local law and feel ashamed after the shower. While you were gone and I was back here something really came out, Bud, that went really far and just didn't quake. We didn't act. That's because I still love you and I'm *sorry* ... we just meant a joke but you're ripping this out of my spleen and I just don't know anymore. But it was all a fucking joke! A joke a joke a joke! It was a whim, it just went out of hand, don't you see? *(Pause. Beverly is broken down on the floor. Bud looks away.)*

BUD. Wynne was right.

BEVERLY. What?

BUD. I washed out, Bev. 'Case you didn't know, I didn't cut it in the marines. They don't dole out honorable discharges to pucker-factors like me. And I come home to this. *(Pause. Bud gets closer to Beverly.)* You know I was there, I was climbing the rope line and my knees swelled up. "Water on the knees." Water on the brain. Jesus. I thought, thought, Bev would kiss my bum knees.

BEVERLY. Bum knees?

BUD. Bum brain.

BEVERLY. Bum brain?

BUD. Bum Bud.

BEVERLY. No. Never. Grunt Bud. Great grunt Bud of his army corners. Sweetie, I — *(Beverly holds her arms out to Bud, who crosses to her.)*

BUD. You *need* me, Bev. I'm what you've wanted. I've had it up to here with the waiting and the joking. Waiting on you. On home. Home is here. It is in you.

BEVERLY. In me.

BUD. In those barracks. Every night. Thought about your skin. Sweat on your necklace. Sweating on me. What about you?

BEVERLY. I've been ... the same.

BUD. And all those nights, and all my nights and yours while tucked, eyes poised on the boob tube, where am I?

BEVERLY. You're away.

BUD. No. I'm right fucking here. And I'm six feet of chestbanging virility. *(He pounds his chest.)* I Bud. You Beverly.

BEVERLY. Right here ... I Beverly.

BUD. Wynne, that goddamned hamstrung, birddoggin' layabout 'n' chickenshit sonofabitch! *(Bud pushes Beverly onto the bed.)*

BEVERLY. ... sonofabitch.

BUD. That cocksuckin' blue-balls anemic.

BEVERLY. Anemic sonofabitch. *(Beverly undoes her blouse and pants.)* You're right, Bud. You're absolutely right.

BUD. I know I am. I'm gonna turn this bed into a spaceship, honey. You and me are gonna have a right galactic fuck.

BEVERLY. Take me, Bud, take me to the galaxy. Show me the sun and the moon. *(Bud summarily takes his pants off and jumps on Beverly. They hump ecstatically. She climaxes right away.)* I would like to introduce the ... seven ... Mercury astronauts: John Glenn ...

BUD. John Glenn.

BEVERLY. Wally Shirra.

BUD. ... Wally ...

BEVERLY. Deke Slayton ...

BUD. ... Slayton.

BEVERLY. Scott Carpenter ...

BUD. ... Scott!

BEVERLY. Alan Shepherd ...

BUD. Alan Shepherd!

BEVERLY. Gus Grissom ...

BUD. ... one for Gus ...

BEVERLY. ... C. Gordon Cooper ...

BUD. Hot dog! ... Yes. Who else?! One more ... Who else?! *Say* it.

BEVERLY. ... and Buddy Combs!

BUD. *(Screams victoriously.)* Ignition! *(Bud and Beverly climax. Pause. Much panting and rolling over.)*

BEVERLY. I need a cigarette.

BUD. Ah. I'm a frontiersman of space. I'm a clean marine. And that ain't no joke.

BEVERLY. We'll have to take these space excursions more often. *(Beverly takes a cigarette out of the night table and lights it, smiles contentedly. Bud leans over and kisses her. He flips on the radio. Something sweet is playing. They cuddle.)* Lovie dove dove.

BUD. Lovie dove dove dove dove.

BEVERLY. My clean marine. *(Beverly runs her hand on Bud's chest. She spots Wynne's tweed hat on the bureau. Pause. She gets up and picks it up, puts it on her head, models it before a stunned Bud. Takes it off, feels it.)* He left this here. He loves this hat so much. *(She is looking at the hat as the lights dim to black.)*

End of Play

83

PROPERTY LIST

Key, suitcase (BUD)
Beer (WYNNE)
Confetti, Welcome Home sign (BEVERLY)
Bourbon, glass (WYNNE)
Cigarette, matches (BEVERLY)

SOUND EFFECTS

Radio love song

NEW PLAYS

★ **MONTHS ON END by Craig Pospisil.** In comic scenes, one for each month of the year, we follow the intertwined worlds of a circle of friends and family whose lives are poised between happiness and heartbreak. "…a triumph…these twelve vignettes all form crucial pieces in the eternal puzzle known as human relationships, an area in which the playwright displays an assured knowledge that spans deep sorrow to unbounded happiness." *–Ann Arbor News.* "…rings with emotional truth, humor…[an] endearing contemplation on love…entertaining and satisfying." *–Oakland Press.* [5M, 5W] ISBN: 0-8222-1892-5

★ **GOOD THING by Jessica Goldberg.** Brings us into the households of John and Nancy Roy, forty-something high-school guidance counselors whose marriage has been increasingly on the rocks and Dean and Mary, recent graduates struggling to make their way in life. "…a blend of gritty social drama, poetic humor and unsubtle existential contemplation…" *–Variety.* [3M, 3W] ISBN: 0-8222-1869-0

★ **THE DEAD EYE BOY by Angus MacLachlan.** Having fallen in love at their Narcotics Anonymous meeting, Billy and Shirley-Diane are striving to overcome the past together. But their relationship is complicated by the presence of Sorin, Shirley-Diane's fourteen-year-old son, a damaged reminder of her dark past. "…a grim, insightful portrait of an unmoored family…" *–NY Times.* "MacLachlan's play isn't for the squeamish, but then, tragic stories delivered at such an unrelenting fever pitch rarely are." *–Variety.* [1M, 1W, 1 boy] ISBN: 0-8222-1844-5

★ **[SIC] by Melissa James Gibson.** In adjacent apartments three young, ambitious neighbors come together to discuss, flirt, argue, share their dreams and plan their futures with unequal degrees of deep hopefulness and abject despair. "A work…concerned with the sound and power of language…" *–NY Times.* "…a wonderfully original take on urban friendship and the comedy of manners—a *Design for Living* for our times…" *–NY Observer.* [3M, 2W] ISBN: 0-8222-1872-0

★ **LOOKING FOR NORMAL by Jane Anderson.** Roy and Irma's twenty-five-year marriage is thrown into turmoil when Roy confesses that he is actually a woman trapped in a man's body, forcing the couple to wrestle with the meaning of their marriage and the delicate dynamics of family. "Jane Anderson's bittersweet transgender domestic comedy-drama …is thoughtful and touching and full of wit and wisdom. A real audience pleaser." *–Hollywood Reporter.* [5M, 4W] ISBN: 0-8222-1857-7

★ **ENDPAPERS by Thomas McCormack.** The regal Joshua Maynard, the old and ailing head of a mid-sized, family-owned book-publishing house in New York City, must name a successor. One faction in the house backs a smart, "pragmatic" manager, the other faction a smart, "sensitive" editor and both factions fear what the other's man could do to this house— and to them. "If Kaufman and Hart had undertaken a comedy about the publishing business, they might have written *Endpapers*…a breathlessly fast, funny, and thoughtful comedy …keeps you amused, guessing, and often surprised…profound in its empathy for the paradoxes of human nature." *–NY Magazine.* [7M, 4W] ISBN: 0-8222-1908-5

★ **THE PAVILION by Craig Wright.** By turns poetic and comic, romantic and philosophical, this play asks old lovers to face the consequences of difficult choices made long ago. "The script's greatest strength lies in the genuineness of its feeling." *–Houston Chronicle.* "Wright's perceptive, gently witty writing makes this familiar situation fresh and thoroughly involving." *–Philadelphia Inquirer.* [2M, 1W (flexible casting)] ISBN: 0-8222-1898-4

DRAMATISTS PLAY SERVICE, INC.
440 Park Avenue South, New York, NY 10016 212-683-8960 Fax 212-213-1539
postmaster@dramatists.com www.dramatists.com

NEW PLAYS

★ **BE AGGRESSIVE by Annie Weisman.** Vista Del Sol is paradise, sandy beaches, avocado-lined streets. But for seventeen-year-old cheerleader Laura, everything changes when her mother is killed in a car crash, and she embarks on a journey to the Spirit Institute of the South where she can learn "cheer" with Bible belt intensity. "…filled with lingual gymnastics…stylized rapid-fire dialogue…" *–Variety.* "…a new, exciting, and unique voice in the American theatre…" *–BackStage West.* [1M, 4W, extras] ISBN: 0-8222-1894-1

★ **FOUR by Christopher Shinn.** Four people struggle desperately to connect in this quiet, sophisticated, moving drama. "…smart, broken-hearted…Mr. Shinn has a precocious and forgiving sense of how power shifts in the game of sexual pursuit…He promises to be a playwright to reckon with…" *–NY Times.* "A voice emerges from an American place. It's got humor, sadness and a fresh and touching rhythm that tell of the loneliness and secrets of life…[a] poetic, haunting play." *–NY Post.* [3M, 1W] ISBN: 0-8222-1850-X

★ **WONDER OF THE WORLD by David Lindsay-Abaire.** A madcap picaresque involving Niagara Falls, a lonely tour-boat captain, a pair of bickering private detectives and a husband's dirty little secret. "Exceedingly whimsical and playfully wicked. Winning and genial. A top-drawer production." *–NY Times.* "Full frontal lunacy is on display. A most assuredly fresh and hilarious tragicomedy of marital discord run amok…absolutely hysterical…" *–Variety.* [3M, 4W (doubling)] ISBN: 0-8222-1863-1

★ **QED by Peter Parnell.** Nobel Prize-winning physicist and all-around genius Richard Feynman holds forth with captivating wit and wisdom in this fascinating biographical play that originally starred Alan Alda. "QED is a seductive mix of science, human affections, moral courage, and comic eccentricity. It reflects on, among other things, death, the absence of God, travel to an unexplored country, the pleasures of drumming, and the need to know and understand." *–NY Magazine.* "Its rhythms correspond to the way that people—even geniuses—approach and avoid highly emotional issues, and it portrays Feynman with affection and awe." *–The New Yorker.* [1M, 1W] ISBN: 0-8222-1924-7

★ **UNWRAP YOUR CANDY by Doug Wright.** Alternately chilling and hilarious, this deliciously macabre collection of four bedtime tales for adults is guaranteed to keep you awake for nights on end. "Engaging and intellectually satisfying…a treat to watch." *–NY Times.* "Fiendishly clever. Mordantly funny and chilling. Doug Wright teases, freezes and zaps us." *–Village Voice.* "Four bite-size plays that bite back." *–Variety.* [flexible casting] ISBN: 0-8222-1871-2

★ **FURTHER THAN THE FURTHEST THING by Zinnie Harris.** On a remote island in the middle of the Atlantic secrets are buried. When the outside world comes calling, the islanders find their world blown apart from the inside as well as beyond. "Harris winningly produces an intimate and poetic, as well as political, family saga." *–Independent (London).* "Harris' enthralling adventure of a play marks a departure from stale, well-furrowed theatrical terrain." *–Evening Standard (London).* [3M, 2W] ISBN: 0-8222-1874-7

★ **THE DESIGNATED MOURNER by Wallace Shawn.** The story of three people living in a country where what sort of books people like to read and how they choose to amuse themselves becomes both firmly personal and unexpectedly entangled with questions of survival. "This is a playwright who does not just tell you what it is like to be arrested at night by goons or to fall morally apart and become an aimless yet weirdly contented ghost yourself. He has the originality to make you feel it." *–Times (London).* "A fascinating play with beautiful passages of writing…" *–Variety.* [2M, 1W] ISBN: 0-8222-1848-8

DRAMATISTS PLAY SERVICE, INC.
440 Park Avenue South, New York, NY 10016 212-683-8960 Fax 212-213-1539
postmaster@dramatists.com   www.dramatists.com

NEW PLAYS

★ **SHEL'S SHORTS by Shel Silverstein.** Lauded poet, songwriter and author of children's books, the incomparable Shel Silverstein's short plays are deeply infused with the same wicked sense of humor that made him famous. "...[a] childlike honesty and twisted sense of humor." *–Boston Herald.* "...terse dialogue and an absurdity laced with a tang of dread give [*Shel's Shorts*] more than a trace of Samuel Beckett's comic existentialism." *–Boston Phoenix.* [flexible casting] ISBN: 0-8222-1897-6

★ **AN ADULT EVENING OF SHEL SILVERSTEIN by Shel Silverstein.** Welcome to the darkly comic world of Shel Silverstein, a world where nothing is as it seems and where the most innocent conversation can turn menacing in an instant. These ten imaginative plays vary widely in content, but the style is unmistakable. "...[*An Adult Evening*] shows off Silverstein's virtuosic gift for wordplay...[and] sends the audience out...with a clear appreciation of human nature as perverse and laughable." *–NY Times.* [flexible casting] ISBN: 0-8222-1873-9

★ **WHERE'S MY MONEY? by John Patrick Shanley.** A caustic and sardonic vivisection of the institution of marriage, laced with the author's inimitable razor-sharp wit. "...Shanley's gift for acid-laced one-liners and emotionally tumescent exchanges is certainly potent..." *–Variety.* "...lively, smart, occasionally scary and rich in reverse wisdom." *–NY Times.* [3M, 3W] ISBN: 0-8222-1865-8

★ **A FEW STOUT INDIVIDUALS by John Guare.** A wonderfully screwy comedy-drama that figures Ulysses S. Grant in the throes of writing his memoirs, surrounded by a cast of fantastical characters, including the Emperor and Empress of Japan, the opera star Adelina Patti and Mark Twain. "Guare's smarts, passion and creativity skyrocket to awesome heights..." *–Star Ledger.* "...precisely the kind of good new play that you might call an everyday miracle...every minute of it is fresh and newly alive..." *–Village Voice.* [10M, 3W] ISBN: 0-8222-1907-7

★ **BREATH, BOOM by Kia Corthron.** A look at fourteen years in the life of Prix, a Bronx native, from her ruthless girl-gang leadership at sixteen through her coming to maturity at thirty. "...vivid world, believable and eye-opening, a place worthy of a dramatic visit, where no one would want to live but many have to." *–NY Times.* "...rich with humor, terse vernacular strength and gritty detail..." *–Variety.* [1M, 9W] ISBN: 0-8222-1849-6

★ **THE LATE HENRY MOSS by Sam Shepard.** Two antagonistic brothers, Ray and Earl, are brought together after their father, Henry Moss, is found dead in his seedy New Mexico home in this classic Shepard tale. "...His singular gift has been for building mysteries out of the ordinary ingredients of American family life..." *–NY Times.* "...rich moments ...Shepard finds gold." *–LA Times.* [7M, 1W] ISBN: 0-8222-1858-5

★ **THE CARPETBAGGER'S CHILDREN by Horton Foote.** One family's history spanning from the Civil War to WWII is recounted by three sisters in evocative, intertwining monologues. "...bittersweet music—[a] rhapsody of ambivalence...in its modest, garrulous way...theatrically daring." *–The New Yorker.* [3W] ISBN: 0-8222-1843-7

★ **THE NINA VARIATIONS by Steven Dietz.** In this funny, fierce and heartbreaking homage to *The Seagull*, Dietz puts Chekhov's star-crossed lovers in a room and doesn't let them out. "A perfect little jewel of a play..." *–Shepherdstown Chronicle.* "...a delightful revelation of a writer at play; and also an odd, haunting, moving theater piece of lingering beauty." *–Eastside Journal (Seattle).* [1M, 1W (flexible casting)] ISBN: 0-8222-1891-7

DRAMATISTS PLAY SERVICE, INC.
440 Park Avenue South, New York, NY 10016   212-683-8960   Fax 212-213-1539
postmaster@dramatists.com   www.dramatists.com